Common Threads: Passion, Perseverance and Praise

The Life Story of Andrew John DeVries, Jr.

www.crookedtreestories.com

Copyright © 2013 by Betty Kuperus Epperly

All rights reserved by the author, including the right of reproduction in whole or in part in any form.

Cover design by Yasmin Ladha

Published by Crooked Tree Stories of Ada, Michigan. Direct inquiries to Crooked Tree Stories @ **www.crookedtreestories.com**.

ISBN 978-1-4825092-1-2

For my dear wife Kay and my friend Chuck Stoddard who gave me continual encouragement to get this done, and to my mentors Bill Carlson, Ken Bootsma and Blake Forslund who provided answers to difficult questions when I faced obstacles.

I would be remiss not to thank all those who came alongside me in my walk through life. In addition to family, I have been surrounded by friends at school, work, and church, and during activities such as playing ball, vacationing, serving on community boards, officiating and mentoring. All of you played an important role in helping me become who I am, and I thank you for doing so.

It is with great joy that I complete this project, and I look forward to reading it with my kids and grandkids. It has provided a chance to relive my life and put it in perspective, to reflect on how passion, perseverance and praise have played out, and to be even more grateful for the life I've been given.

Life is But a Weaving

My life is but a weaving, between my God and me.
I cannot choose the colors; He weaveth steadily.
Oft' times He weaveth sorrow, and I in foolish pride
Forget He sees the upper, and I the underside.
Not 'til the loom is silent and the shuttles cease to fly,
Will God unroll the canvas and reveal the reason why.
The dark threads are as needful in the weaver's skillful hand,
As the threads of gold and silver in the pattern He has planned.
He knows, He loves, He cares; nothing this truth can dim.
He gives the very best to those who leave the choice to Him.

- Corrie Ten Boom

Table of Contents

Chapter 1: Dutch Roots	7
Chapter 2: Early Days on 10th Street	13
Chapter 3: World War II: Service and Sacrifice	19
Chapter 4: A Growing Family	31
Chapter 5: Teenage Years	71
Chapter 6: Independence and Higher Learning	87
Chapter 7: Marriage and Responsibilities	103
Chapter 8: Kids of Our Own and Career Changes	117
Chapter 9: Brushes With Death Bring Abundant Life	153
Chapter 10: Ties That Bind: Passion, Perseverance and Praise	177
Chapter 11: Perspective in a Nutshell	189
Bibliography	207
History of Dutch Surnames	208
Grand Rapids Press Article	210
Alums Support "Average Joe"	213

Foreward

I met Andy DeVries at a Christmas party in 2012 for Excel Charter Academy. Through initial chitchat we discovered commonalities – a deep respect for the school, Dutch immigrant ancestors, and a connection to Calvin College. Beyond that, we spoke of how our lives had taken unexpected twists and turns. Andy's story blew me away, and I asked if he'd considered writing his life story.

Andy's story is remarkable, in part, because he has boldly lived his life to the fullest; he has made unconventional choices and defied many odds; he has championed the underdog in many walks of life; he has invested deeply in relationships and community. But what makes him an outlier is that, in the face of extreme challenges and brushes with death, Andy has chosen hope, always with the faith that something good is yet to come.

The theme of a common thread came up often as Andy told his story. Relationships and experiences in a healthy community are interwoven and indelibly connected. The backside of a tapestry is chaotic and every flaw is visible. Life can be hard, and pain and loss are often the messy backstories. But if we flip the tapestry over, the patterns coalesce and bring clarity. Just as knots and tangles add texture to the fabric, our lives can be more rich and meaningful when we push through hardships and mistakes. By the grace of God we can say that our lives contribute to a narrative that extends beyond ourselves.

Andy is a straight shooter. He tells his life story with humor, candor and conviction. His powerful life lessons resonated with me, and I am confident that all who read his story will be inspired and touched.

- Betty Kuperus Epperly, July 2013

Dutch Roots

"Give me your tired, your poor, your huddled masses yearning to breathe free, the wretched refuse of your teeming shore. Send these, the homeless, tempest-tossed to me, I lift my lamp beside the golden door!" – *"The New Colossus" by Emma Lazarus.*

On his deathbed in 1901 my Dutch great-grandfather had one request for his youngest son, my grandfather John DeVries: that he travel across the Atlantic Ocean to Grand Rapids, Michigan, in order to check on his older brother Johannes.

Jan (John) Andries DeVries, my paternal grandfather, was born on July 13, 1883, to Andries Pieters DeVries and Leelke Tjeerds Annema DeVries. Andries was fifty-two years old when Grandpa, the youngest of his ten children, was born. The DeVries family were bakers, and while the older brothers continued in this vocation, there was no room in the business for the younger sons.

Young John finally traveled to America six years later, after his mother passed away.

Brother Johannes, eleven years older than John, had immigrated to America in 1897. He seems to have been the prodigal of the family, and the reason for my great-grandfather's deathbed wish stemmed from concern that Johannes had a problem with alcohol.

My grandfather boarded the *S.S. Ryndam* in Rotterdam with the equivalent of forty dollars in his pocket and arrived on Ellis Island, New York, on April 3, 1907. This act in itself shows his incredible bravery. He knew no English, yet he was willing to take an enormous risk by staking a claim in an unknown country, entering the Land of Promise perhaps feeling that he had little to offer.

The S.S. Ryndam, circa 1910.

The S.S. Ryndam was built by Harland & Wolff of Belfast, Ireland, in 1901 for the Holland America Line. She was 550.3 feet long by 62.3 feet high with one funnel, two masts, twin screw and a speed of 15 knots. There was accommodation for 286-1st, 196-2nd and 1,800-3rd class passengers.

Launched on May 18, 1901, she commenced her maiden voyage from Rotterdam to New York on October 10, 1901. On January 18, 1916, she was damaged by a mine in the North Sea, repaired in Rotterdam and resumed the Rotterdam to New York service on April 15, 1916. On December 3, 1918, she was requisitioned by the United States government for transport services but resumed the Rotterdam to New York service on July 31, 1920.

Dutch Roots

In May 1925 she was refitted to carry cabin and 3rd class passengers. She commenced her last Rotterdam to New York voyage on April 16, 1929, and was scrapped the same year at Hendrik Ido Ambacht on the island of IJsselmonde, near Rotterdam. [1]

Johannes DeVries lived at 310 Alpine Avenue in Grand Rapids with his wife, Engelte, and their children. According to the 1900 census, Johannes was a lumber worker. As noted in the 1910 census, his family was living at 201 Quarry Street, and Johannes' occupation was listed as factory teamster.

After John made his journey to America he resided with his brother, and the 1910 census notes that he was a peddler/huckster. He would go up and down the streets selling his wares from his horse and buggy. For seven years John DeVries worked to save money and make a life, and in 1914 he returned to the Netherlands.

John DeVries in front of his huckster wagon, circa 1910.

The purpose of my grandfather's return to his homeland was to marry Saakje Mients Bouma. Born on August 11, 1887, Saakje was four years younger than her new husband. Like my grandfather, she was also from a family of ten children. Saakje's father, Mient Mients Bouma, a wealthy merchant, was very much opposed to the union, and had sent John a letter suggesting that he find a different young lady to marry.

My grandfather ignored this advice. He and Saakje were married on April 2, 1914, and rather than lingering to celebrate, they boarded a ship to the United States the day after they were wed. As was common for European immigrants, American officials persuaded Saakje to choose an American name, so she changed hers to Sylvia. The newlyweds experienced heartache when their daughter, Josephine Sylvia, died at six months old on June 4, 1915. A son was stillborn on January 25, 1917.

A home was built at 860 10th Street using salvaged wood from Alpine Avenue Christian Reformed Church, which had sustained a fire in 1914.

After the fire: Alpine Avenue Christian Reformed Church, 1914.

Saakje would be the only member of the Bouma family to immigrate to the United States. Especially because of her father's opposition, there was a

Dutch Roots

pressure to succeed in this new land.

The young couple expanded their fledgling business. John continued to peddle goods while his new bride operated a dry goods store from the ground floor of their two-story building.

The sign above their store advertised "Cash and Carry Groceries" and prominently displayed their telephone number, as did Grandpa's huckster wagon.

According to 1920 census records their surname was spelled "DeFries." In the 1930 census it was listed as "DeVries." My grandfather was short in stature, and although my grandmother was only slightly taller, he stood on a platform or step whenever they were photographed together.

Early Days on 10th Street

"Remember, remember always, that all of us, and you and I especially, are descended from immigrants and revolutionists." - Franklin D. Roosevelt

In the early 20th century in towns such as Grand Rapids it was common to see a small grocery store on every block. In her store Grandma used a coffee grinder to grind beans to the customer's specifications. Every day a deliveryman placed a big block of ice in a special compartment of the tin-lined icebox. Grandma sold no frozen goods, just milk, eggs and other dairy products, which my grandfather had previously sold from his wagon.

Grandma would try to anticipate the daily needs of her customers, so she might also have on hand a couple of pounds of hamburger and maybe a chicken or two. Any meat that was not sold by the end of the business day would be prepared for supper.

Dry goods such as cereal and flour were stored in cans on a shelf. She had a huge display of penny candy: cards of candy "pills," sugary watermelon slices, Chum gum, Mary Jane peanut butter chews, Black Jack taffy and red

Common Threads: Passion, Perseverance and Praise

licorice strings. Pez candy dispensers and packages of Topps baseball cards that came with pink bubble gum cost a nickel.

While Grandma ran the store, Grandpa continued peddling. He woke at 4:00 a.m., drove his horse and wagon to the farmers market at Leonard Street and the Grand River, loaded up his cart with fruits and vegetables, and sold his goods on the streets of the Alpine/Leonard area.

Leonard Street Farmers Market, 1920.

My grandfather was thirty years old when my father, Andrew John DeVries, was born on January 19, 1918. Another son, Monroe ("Bud"), was born on December 29, 1919. A daughter, Leona, was born on April 23, 1923, but died on October 9, 1924.

Although Jan and Saakje DeVries never returned to their country of origin, letters and pictures were exchanged with family members who remained in the Netherlands. In photographs the children were dressed in fine clothing to create the illusion of prosperity. In reality, although they were comfortable and had enough food to eat, they were by no means wealthy.

Despite the language barrier, Grandpa was able to display tremendous perseverance and resilience. His work ethic was always evident, especially when times were tough. During the economic depression of the 1930s he was gracious to his customers. If they had no money he would give them food and run tabs, some of which were never paid.

For a time my grandparents took in a boarder for extra income, despite their tiny living quarters. Aukje Plantinga lived with the DeVries family for many years. Despite busy workdays, Aukje, Grandpa DeVries and my father enjoyed reprieves at the Grand Haven beach. Aukje's tombstone is next to the DeVries plots in Washington Park Memorial Cemetery on Richmond Avenue in Walker Township. My grandfather paid for Mr. Plantinga's funeral and burial expenses.

It was important to my grandparents, as it was to many Dutch families, that their sons attend the local Christian school. This was a tremendous financial sacrifice. My grandma would sew a quarter (the weekly tuition) in my father's pants pocket each Monday morning to ensure that he wouldn't lose it on the way to the school office. Although they attended Grand Rapids Christian High School, neither my father nor Bud would graduate because they needed to contribute to the family's income by doing any odd jobs that were available.

Andy and Bud DeVries, 1928.

My father matured early and was large in stature, and legend has it that while he was not one to start fights, he could effectively end them. Although he showed signs of being a good athlete, he did not have the opportunity to become involved in sports.

Bud and Andy DeVries, Sr. assisting in the family business.

Along with assisting his mom and dad in their business, my father, at the age of sixteen, helped to build the highway between Grand Rapids and Lansing, well before child labor laws were established.

Andy DeVries Sr. behind the wheel of a friend's Model T. Ford, circa 1934.

Early Days on 10th Street

Cars were a luxury in those days, and although my dad's family did not own one, he and several friends each chipped in $2.00 and bought a junker for a total of $10.00. The car required many repairs, but when it finally ran the boys had loads of fun, so it was money well spent.

My mother's ancestors were also Dutch immigrants from the province of Friesland. Her parents, Albert and Beatrice (Kuiper) Rodenhouse, owned a farm at 3 Mile Road and Walker in the area that is now the Meijer corporate offices. Since this was so far from Grand Rapids Christian High School and there was no viable transportation service to and from the school, Mom lived with her grandparents, whose home was close to the high school. It was in high school that my parents fell in love.

World War II put an end to my father's relatively carefree days. He and his brother Bud both received commissions on the battlefield, but in very different capacities. The advent of the war precipitated many weddings; sometimes the young women felt sorry for soldiers who were shipping out. Sometimes marriage was appealing to forge a deeper connection while the couple was separated. Before my father departed for duty to Europe, he married my mother, Bertha Jeane Rodenhouse, in October of 1942.

Newlyweds Bud and Doris DeVries, 1942.

World War II: Service and Sacrifice

"As I walked the beaches of Normandy with the American veterans who had returned for this anniversary and listened to their stories, I was deeply moved and profoundly grateful for all they had done. Ten years later, I returned to Normandy for the fiftieth anniversary of the invasion, and by then I had come to understand what this generation of Americans meant to history. It is, I believe, the greatest generation any society has ever produced." - Tom Brokaw

My father achieved the rank of captain as a commander in a tank corp. Although he spoke very little of his experiences, we do know that he participated in the Battle of the Bulge, one of the turning points for the Allied Army.

Common Threads: Passion, Perseverance and Praise

The Battle of the Bulge

In December 1944 Adolf Hitler ordered the only major German counteroffensive of the war in northwest Europe. Its objective was to split the Allied armies by means of a surprise blitzkrieg thrust through the Ardennes Mountains to Antwerp, Belgium. Despite Germany's historical penchant for mounting counteroffensives when things looked darkest, the Allies' leadership miscalculated and left the Ardennes lightly defended by only two inexperienced and battered American divisions.

On December 16, more than a quarter-million German troops launched the deadliest and most desperate battle of the war in the west in the rugged, heavily forested Ardennes. The once-quiet region became bedlam as American units fought desperate battles to stem the German advance.

The inexperienced U.S. 106th Division was nearly annihilated, but this helped buy time for Brigadier General Bruce C. Clarke's brilliant defense of St.-Vith. As the German armies drove deeper into the Ardennes, the line defining the Allied front took on the appearance of a large protrusion or bulge, the name by which the battle would forever be known.

A crucial German shortage of fuel and the gallantry of American soldiers proved fatal to Hitler's ambition to snatch, if not a victory, at least a draw with the Allies in the west. Lieutenant General George S. Patton's remarkable feat of turning the Third Army ninety degrees from Lorraine to relieve the besieged town of Bastogne was the key to thwarting the German counteroffensive. The Battle of the Bulge was the costliest action ever fought by the U.S. Army, which suffered over 100,000 casualties. [2]

General George S. Patton

I have to wonder how my mother coped during my father's absence, knowing that he was in harm's way every day. She found work as a nurse during the war, once with General Motors in industrial nursing. When factory workers were injured they were sent to her. She told stories of accidents, such as when upholstery seamstresses accidentally sewed one of their fingers to a piece of fabric.

World War II: Sacrifice and Service

Grandma DeVries receives word from a mail carrier about her sons.

While Dad was tapped for officer training, Uncle Bud was assigned to the U.S. Army Veterinary Corp. Mules and horses were used during World War II to carry ammunition and supplies, move cannons, and navigate difficult terrain. Uncle Bud was also involved in the crossing of the Rhine at the end of the war.

The Crossing of the Rhine

After the Battle of the Bulge, Germany was the next target. It was clear to everyone but the most fanatical Nazis, including Hitler, that Germany was finished.

Throughout February and March 1945, the Allies fought their way through the **Siegfried Line***, a series of antitank fortifications, pillboxes, and artillery that ran along the Western border with Germany. Manned by young boys and old men, the Siegfried Line was a tough line that held the Allies out of Germany since September.*

The Allies advanced and captured Cologne, the first major German city, on March 5, 1945. US Army General Dwight D. Eisenhower, commanding the Allied forces, realized that the capture of Berlin was secondary to destroying the German military industrial machine. Churchill, especially, wanted the Allies to capture Berlin, but Eisenhower had enough of long narrow advances in Holland. The Allies would cross the Rhine and advance on the Ruhr.

Hitler saw the Rhine as a symbol of German resolve. No invading army had crossed the Rhine in 140 years, since Napoleon in 1805. Any commander surrendering or retreating would be shot. Bridges were to be blown up. Cologne's bridges were thus destroyed before the city was captured.

The Allies rushed to cross the Rhine under air and artillery attack. By March 23 the Allies had a bridgehead thirty-five mile wide and twelve miles deep. Bridges were put up over the Rhine by special bridge units, many of which were segregated black units. Often the crossings were under heavy German fire.

Crossing the Rhine. Photo courtesy of Bud DeVries

Allied airborne forces, in the last operation in Europe, dropped over the Rhine on March 25 in Operation Varsity on March 24, 1945. German antiaircraft units were waiting and casualties were heavy, but the paratroopers landed together and took the East bank of the Rhine to protect the bridgehead.

WWII "Long Tom" 155 mm caliber field gun. Photo courtesy of Bud DeVries.

The Rhine had been cracked. Bridges were quickly constructed all over the Rhine, more than sixty in total. Hitler was unable to stop the Allies in the west.

World War II: Sacrifice and Service

The Red Army was advancing in the East; Berlin was their next and final target.[3]

My mom's brother Al, although willing to serve in the war effort, received a medical exemption because of a foot problem. Uncle Ken was assigned to the Coast Guard and served stateside. Uncle Bob became a B-17 and B-29 pilot, belonging to a squad that dropped the atom bomb on Hiroshima and effectively ended the war.

PBS: Victory in the Pacific

In September 1942 the Boeing Company scheduled the first test flight of its new B-29 bomber. But it would be early 1944 before the Army Air Forces received the airplane for use against the Japanese. The B-29, or Superfortress, as it was called, was designed to operate faster, at higher altitudes, and with heavier bomb loads than its predecessor, the B-17 Flying Fortress.

Boeing B-29 bombers

*Considered the **most advanced bombers** in the world, the B-29s had pressurized cabins, remote control gun placements and 2,200-horsepower engines -- the most powerful piston engines of the time. Able to fly over 3,000 miles, up to 16 hours, these bombers were just what the Allies needed to target Japan. As Robert Rodenhouse, a B-29 pilot, remembers:*

23

"It just blew my mind. First of all its size, and then its capabilities. And to think that they could take an airplane, a bomber, and pressurize it so that we could feel the same at sea level as we do at 30,000 feet. And that's essentially what they were doing. And then when I knew that the range that it was capable of doing, and the weight and the bomb load, I couldn't wait to get behind the wheel."

Lieutenant Commander Robert Rodenhouse

In April 1944, the American Joint Chiefs of Staff approved a plan they code named "Matterhorn." B-29 bombers would attack Japan from China. On their first mission on June 14, 1944, sixty B-29s attacked iron and steel factories on the Japanese island of Kyushu without success. Enemy attacks on bases and long distance fuel runs would plague the program in China.

The first B-29s arrived in the Mariana Islands in October 1944. This base was closer to Japan, but the bombing runs still had problems. The B-29s had been rushed into service without complete testing. The result was not good, according to Rodenhouse:

"We had trouble even getting the bomb bay doors to retract, and also the landing gear. The biggest problem was overheating of engines. And that was so critical, because if an engine coughed or sputtered on a takeoff, you'll never make it. You'll never get off the ground. And the plane was so overloaded that it would never be able to stop it with its normal braking."

*The planes **were hard to handle.** Heavy bomb loads made takeoffs risky. Flying 3,000 miles round trip to Japan over hostile waters made emergency landings almost impossible. But perhaps the most baffling problem to the flight crews was something we know today as the "jet stream."*

"If we were going with the jet stream, our bombs were going over the target. And if we're going against it, the bombs would be short of the target. And it wasn't until about three or four missions that some meteorologist went along with the bombing group, and they determined what that was, a jet stream," recalled Rodenhouse. "It's a very common occurrence now. It's in every meteorological broadcast today, where the jet stream is, and how fast it is, and what it's moving. It has such an effect on weather systems. And we didn't know about that."

In January 1945, General Curtis LeMay arrived in the Mariana Islands to take over the problem-plagued B-29 command. For two months, his crews flew similar high-altitude missions over Japan with little more success. His job on the line, General LeMay decided on a risky new strategy: his pilots would fly daring, dangerous bombing missions at altitudes as low as 5,000 feet, low enough to be within range of anti-aircraft weapons. Robert Rodenhouse was shocked:

"We thought they could throw the kitchen sink up there and hit us. Can you imagine flying a big four-engine bomber at 5,000 feet? Why that was just unheard of, absolutely unheard of. And like my crew says, I think those generals lost their marbles. They weren't thinking straight."

The low-altitude bombing runs turned out to be highly successful. The planes carried much larger bomb loads. Crews flew at night to avoid enemy fighters. And flight personnel were kept to a minimum. Most of the gunners were removed to make room for still more bombs -- incendiary bombs. Incendiary bombs were composed of gelatinized gasoline, known as napalm. When incendiaries hit the target, the napalm started fires that spread quickly and were almost impossible to extinguish. Japanese cities were mostly made out of wood and paper, so the fires created infernos.

On March 10, 1945, flying in darkness at low altitudes, more than 300 B-29s dropped close to a quarter of a million incendiary bombs over Tokyo. LeMay's gamble was successful. Perhaps as many as 100,000 Japanese were dead, almost 16 square miles of the city destroyed, and a million people homeless.

Not all the B-29 crews made it back safely to their home bases. As war prisoners in Japanese hands, some of the men suffered unimaginable hardships. In some cases they were executed immediately, but in others they were submitted to various forms of torture including medical experimentation, beheading, cannibalism, and even death by being burnt alive. One captured B-29 flyer was put on display at a zoo in Tokyo. It is not known exactly how many downed B-29 flyers were killed while being held prisoner, but the numbers reach into the hundreds.[4]

Tom Brokaw produced a documentary for NBC in 1984 about WWII and was so profoundly affected by the sacrifices of these men and women that he was inspired to write a book called <u>The Greatest Generation</u>. Uncle Bob was further quoted in the film *Victory in the Pacific* (which can be viewed on pbs.com).

Toward the end of war, my father was involved in liberating the concentration camps, and when the war ended in 1945 he was asked to continue his service in the occupation army that stayed in Germany. Although the United States government had also made provisions for a free college education for World War II soldiers in the GI Bill of Rights, my father and my uncles probably felt immense pressure to support their families, so the luxury of college was not an option.

The G.I. Bill of Rights

The GI Bill of Rights was signed into law on June 22, 1944, by President Franklin D. Roosevelt. Few people were aware of the implications of this revolutionary new law. Commentary tended to stress the benefits of the unemployment allowance and to underestimate the education and loan program provisions.

For educational benefits, the VA paid tuition, fees, and books, and provided a monthly living stipend. For home loans, the VA guaranteed a portion of the loan to the lending institution at a low 4 percent interest.

Among the legacies of the GI Bill is the belief that education was available to anyone, regardless of age, sex, race or religion. Millions of vets had not even graduated from grammar school. Only 23% had a high school diploma and 3% had college degrees.

It is estimated that approximately half of the 16,000,000 WWII veterans took advantage of this provision to receive a college education. These graduates raised expectations throughout the country, and their skilled labor contributed to a literate middle class.

By the early 1970s, one in five Americans had a college education, compared to one in 16 prior to the war. The GI Bill led to enormous social change. Views regarding sex, religion, and race were shaken up.

About 64,000 women took advantage of the bill's education opportunities. Jewish veterans gained entry into many schools that had previously rejected them. Many black veterans were turned away from overly crowded black institutions and yet could not attend white southern schools.

During the 16 years of depression and war, it was not just the lack of new housing, but also that existing homes had fallen into disrepair. After World War II building resumed, but materials were in short supply.

By the end of 1947, the VA guaranteed over one million loans for homes and businesses. Under the VA Loan, the government co-signed half of a veteran's mortgage. This encouraged developers to build and bankers to lend, often with no down payment.

What the GI Bill represented is that a national commitment to mobility pays dividends for both individuals and the nation. The GI Bill enabled the nation to overcome instability, restored human, economic, and social capital, and helped catapult the U.S. to leadership on the world's stage.[5]

Uncle Bud contacted my father with an opportunity to buy a coal company that was owned by Bud's father-in-law. Dad turned down the offer to stay with the occupation army, and Mol-DeVries Coal Company was in business.

Although my father jumped back into civilian life when he came home in 1946, he probably felt like he returned to a totally different country. I believe that his war experiences had a profound effect on him. My mother had married a pretty happy-go-lucky guy, but he came back a changed man who did not communicate what he had experienced. The term "Post-traumatic Stress Syndrome" had not yet been coined, but many soldiers bottled up things they had undergone, and as a result carried a lot of angst for the rest of their lives.

Bud DeVries poses with truck salesman, circa 1950.

As was true on my father's side, it was important for my mother's family to be involved in business, which was a legacy that would carry over to my cousins and me. There are pictures of Grandpa Rodenhouse bucking hay in the Dakotas when he was younger, before hay bales existed. He used to talk about "riding the rails," and I'd love to know what he meant by that. It may have involved jumping on a boxcar in Grand Rapids and riding it with the hobos until he found a suitable place for work.

Besides running his farm in the Grand Rapids area, Grandpa Rodenhouse showed initiative by starting an orange grove in Florida, which he would tend in the winters. He was a true entrepreneur, on the forefront of building and developing. His company, Rodenhouse Door and Window, built solid bungalows on the southwest side for soldiers returning from the war. In fact, one street off of Division on which he built many homes bears my mom's first name, Jean.

Even though Uncle Al did not serve in the war, he put his entrepreneurial sense to work and had an innovative idea. Realizing that returning soldiers would need homes, he bought what amounted to an entire shipload of nails. This became West Michigan Nail and Wire. His timing was right and his gamble paid off; the business experienced phenomenal success.

Uncle Ken was always peddling and selling something. Over the years he had a feed store, a rent-to-own place, and even a car lot.

The Rodenhouse philosophy seemed to be "If you're going to do it, do it right." Don't be afraid to go into business; you may not be successful, but you've got to try. Another tenet was character. Above the doorframe of the entrance to Grandpa's business was a reference to Proverbs 22:1 – "A good name is rather to be chosen than great riches, and loving favor rather than silver and gold."

Both my parents' families were self-reliant. Because of their culture, their history, and the struggles they endured, they developed strength of character. Their can-do spirit and work ethic was borne of necessity. They did not accept handouts from the government and did not indulge in self-pity. The modeling of these characteristics turned out to be a huge piece of who I am today, although it was not something I would fully appreciate until much later in life.

Common Threads: Passion, Perseverance and Praise

A Growing Family

"All of us grow up in particular realities - a home, family, a clan, a small town, a neighborhood. Depending upon how we're brought up, we are either deeply aware of the particular reading of reality into which we are born, or we are peripherally aware of it."- Chaim Potok

My grandparents allowed my parents to make a home in the apartment above their store on 10th Street. I was born on March 9, 1947. Our home was essentially one big room; I don't remember any walls. To divide the space, a curtain was hung over a wire that hung from the ceiling.

Andy DeVries Jr., Andy DeVries Sr., and Jeane DeVries, 1949.

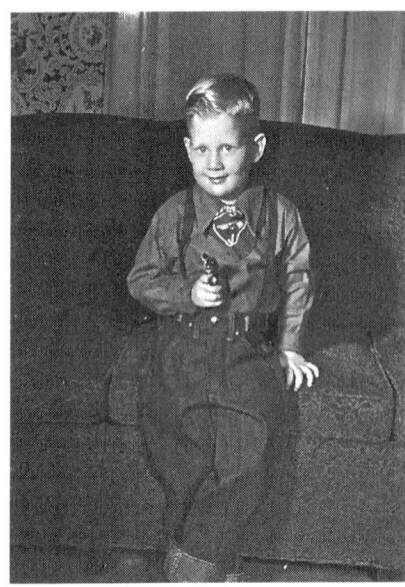

Little Sheriff Andy, ready for a duel.

The living area behind the store became my grandparents' new home, consisting of a kitchen, a tiny living room, a bedroom and a bathroom. I remember the snugness and warmth of my grandparents' bed when I occasionally slept with them. Every day I made countless trips up and down those stairs. One of my first memories is when, at the age of three, I was hurt badly when I fell down the stairs. It was Grandma who gave me comfort.

In this three-generation photograph, Grandpa DeVries (sixty-one years old) is holding me (one year old), and my father, seated behind us, is thirty-one years old:

A Growing Family

I remember that Grandma's store was always busy, and she never sat down. A highlight for me was when I helped her stock the penny candy bins. Grandma did not take no for an answer and never quit, even when faced with obstacles. She ran the family in a firm manner, but I would say that I learned the art of loving from her. Grandma was a strong presence in my early life.

Four generations: Great-grandfather Kuiper, Grandma Rodenhouse, Andy DeVries Jr., and my mom, Jeane DeVries.

Beneath the main floor was a standard Michigan basement that had a huge coal furnace. The basement was not finished, but had angled walls that were covered in plaster. Grandpa was relegated to this area to smoke his ubiquitous pipe. He spent countless hours sitting in his rocking chair and reading his Bible. An old Campbell's soup can nailed to the top of the chair served as a headrest.

A barn behind the store and residence contained half a dozen stalls in which Grandpa kept a horse that pulled his cart. Later the barn housed his truck, which eventually took the place of his horse and wagon. Legend has it that he never did learn to drive properly. He used to hit a lot of trees and other inanimate objects, but the police looked the other way.

When he was not peddling or enjoying his quiet time, Grandpa was always tinkering. In a lean-to at the back of the barn was a workbench where he fashioned makeshift tools and fixed whatever needed fixing.

Since my grandpa never became fluent in English, I never felt that I knew him very well. He knew just enough to get by in his huckster business, selling produce in the neighborhoods on the west side of Grand Rapids. I remember him singing in his Dutch brogue as he went up and down the streets: "Str-a-a-wberries! Ra-a-a-spberries! Pota-a-a-toes!" When people heard him, they would come out of their houses to shop at his mobile market. To his credit, Grandpa found time to learn how to play an instrument and belonged to a community band.

In 1949 our family moved a few blocks away to a three-bedroom two-story house at 1039 11th Street. After years of sleeping in my parents' room, I had a room of my very own, and I'll never forget how special that felt.

A Growing Family

Our family grew quickly; Sharon Leone was born on May 17, 1949, and another daughter, Donna Jean, joined us on September 30, 1950. My mom had her hands full with three kids in quick succession. For momentary relief she would pay me to pull my sisters around the block in a wagon.

Uncle Bud and Aunt Doris' five children were born during the same time period, so we spent lots of time with our cousins.

The DeVries clan pictured in front of 1039 11th Street: cousin John, Andy Jr., cousin Alice, cousin Joan, sister Sharon, and sister Donna, circa 1953.

Like my parents, we attended Christian schools. Our home was within walking distance of West Side Christian, where Grandma Rodenhouse had taught before she had children. I was only four years old when I started kindergarten, but I am guessing that my parents enrolled me early to get me out of the house. My neighbor Kenny Koppenol escorted me on the first day. Kenny was about four years older and occasionally babysat for us, and I thought he was pretty cool.

My sense of adventure got the best of me even as a youngster. When I was in first grade the 7th Reformed Church (on the corner of Leonard and Tamarack) was building an addition. One day I rode my bike to the construction site instead of going to school. I noticed some pipes that had been laid in the ground and wondered where they led, so I proceeded to crawl through them.

It was not long before I got stuck. The school, noticing my absence, called my mom, who recruited Kenny to help with the search. He spotted my bike leaning against the church and soon discovered my feet protruding from a pipe. From the moment that he delivered me, Kenny instantly achieved hero status in my eyes. (I am convinced that my claustrophobia is rooted in that event.)

Andy DeVries Jr., 1954.

School was something that I endured so that I could get outside and do the things that I really loved to do. Ironically, Grandma DeVries, who barely spoke English, became one of my greatest motivators. I would go to her house to complain (because she was the only one who would listen) about the difficulty of the spelling words, claiming that it was pointless to learn words that I would never use in a sentence.

"Nonsense," she said. "*We* will learn these words together."

So Grandma learned English through helping me with my spelling words. One of the words we learned was "conscientiousness," and ironically, it was on that word that I later won an all-school spelling bee.

Once a week after school I'd play chess with Grandpa. Despite the fact that he did not speak English, he was still able to teach me how to play.

My parents felt that it was important that their children understood the Bible; Scripture and prayer were a part of every meal. On Sundays we attended morning and evening church services, and we attended catechism class on Mondays after school. Dad was very involved in civic organizations, and if people wanted to get things done they came to him. After the Korean conflict in the late 1950s it seemed that we had a missionary or pastor from Korea at our home every Sunday. Although Dad turned down an opportunity to become involved in the Korean War, he was involved in clothing and food drives through the Christian Reformed Church.

Andy DeVries Sr. holds the right of the sign.

In observing my parents' marriage I scarcely recall tenderness, just acceptance. I believe that my father would have appreciated a college education, and perhaps he realized that this window had closed for him. He was a voracious reader of cerebral materials, opting for Melville, Thoreau, and Aristotle. Although he was well read and had the intelligence of an officer, his speech belied him; he still had the grammar of a blue-collar west side guy.

My father gave generously of his time to others, but he kept his kids at a distance. He did take me to some local ball games. We went canoeing once, and he occasionally took me fishing. My extreme interest in sports probably seemed trivial to him, although I do remember playing catch with him a couple of times. I once missed one of his throws and took it in the face. The cost to replace my broken glasses put the kabash on repeat performances. At this time it seemed that something changed in him, and he kind of checked out as a father. Thankfully, at about this same time, Cadets kicked in.

The Cadet Club, our church's version of Boy Scouts, met on Wednesday evenings, and I absolutely loved it. We had opportunities to earn merit badges, and I learned so much about the outdoors. On campouts, ours was the rowdiest church group, but despite our naughtiness we were great campers and we knew how to pull it together. To our counselors' consternation, it was our rambunctious group that came away with the awards.

Besides learning about camping and hunting, one thing that we made was crystal radios. We'd tune into a station by pulling a bar out from a cylinder. Bedtime, even on Saturday nights, was 8:00 p.m., and I did not argue, but when it was lights off, the Calvin College basketball game came on. Some Sunday afternoons I picked up Detroit Tiger baseball.

Sundays were set aside as a day of rest. Grandpa and Grandma DeVries would come to our house after church, and my mom always cooked a nice dinner.

Somehow Grandma was able to come across some silver dollars. Instead of spending money on herself she used this money to encourage her grandchildren to memorize the Heidelberg Catechism. It meant a lot to my grandparents to contribute to our theological foundation.

After Sunday dinner Grandma would ask, "Does anybody have a Lord's Day?" If we could recite a question and answer verbatim, she would allow us to choose one of her silver dollars. I have kept those silver dollars, and the words of the catechism are still with me as well, and have come back to me during difficult times in my life.

My sisters and I would put on a program for the adults in the living room. (This was the only occasion for which the living room was ever used.) I played solos on my baritone, and the girls played the piano. Grandma and Grandpa always sat back and smiled. We played from a big book of songs from which they would make requests. They were especially fond of "*I Come to the Garden Alone When the Dew is Still on the Roses*" and "*Holy City*." When Grandma and Grandpa Rodenhouse joined us they requested "*God Be With You Till We Meet Again,*" which now has a special significance.

Following these recitals, it was naptime for the adults. My sisters also took naps, but I had other plans. After the house was quiet I'd sneak out the window onto the short roof, jump down and play with my Catholic friends until it was time for evening church. My sisters would leave the basement window open for me, and I'd crawl through and find something to read until the rest of the house woke up.

Once in a while we'd get in the car to visit Grandma and Grandpa Rodenhouse on Lake Michigan Drive. They had a nice house in the country on a big lot, surrounded by apple and peach trees, raspberry bushes and a vegetable garden. Sometimes I would ride my bike to their house to mow Grandpa's lawn, which took most of the day because of its size. He rewarded my work with wages. Grandpa always had nice cars. His Oldsmobiles and Cadillacs were symbols of prosperity. A common treat for his grandchildren was chocolate-covered raisins, and he often pulled a half-dollar from his pocket to give to us.

Grandma and Grandpa Rodenhouse would often be our guests for Saturday dinner. Dad would cook on these occasions, and he made great hamburgers. For dessert, we'd have ice cream, a rare treat since our refrigerator did not have a freezer. I'd buy a pint at Bylsma's Dairy or Stapletons and run all the way back before the ice cream had a chance to melt.

I couldn't wait for the school year to end; summer meant freedom. Dad would rent a cottage on Big Star Lake or Crockery Lake for a week. Mom would spend most of her time reading, and my sisters and I just had each other. Out of boredom we'd challenge each other to swim across the lake. Mom would be very upset, but I always came back. I'd row my sisters around the lake in our little boat and try to get them to reciprocate.

Grandma and Grandpa DeVries and their grandkids, 1956.

A Growing Family

Dad would occasionally come to the lake after work. When I was about ten years old he brought out a Chris-Craft 10-horse outboard motor for the rowboat and we'd fish at night. I talked him into teaching me how to run the motor so I could take it around the lake in his absence during the days.

Dad loved to play board games, and almost every night we'd play Monopoly. My sister Sharon would sit on some of her money, and just when you thought you had her, she'd pull a $500 bill out of nowhere.

Grandma and Grandpa Rodenhouse visit us at Big Star Lake.

At one time there was a huge train hub in downtown Grand Rapids on Bridge Street. Since Grandma and Grandpa DeVries had no car they took the train to Baldwin, and we picked them up at the station. Although it was less than a hundred miles from their home to Big Star Lake, it may have been the longest trip they'd taken as a married couple aside from their voyage across the Atlantic Ocean. At the lake, Grandpa rocked in his chair and Grandma sat on the shore with us.

Grandpa DeVries was thirty years old when my dad was born and my dad was thirty years old when I was born, so my grandparents were in their seventies at this point. I remember them as kind and watchful grandparents, but they were not very interactive. After working hard for so many years they probably just enjoyed relaxation and solitude. Grandpa DeVries occasionally went fishing on the Grand Haven pier, still dressed to a tee.

My mom and I rode with Uncle Ken and Aunt Ruth to Grandpa Rodenhouse's orange grove in Florida in 1956. Along the way we stayed in tourist rooms, a forerunner of the hostel. People would open their homes to travelers. We were given a bedroom but had to share a bathroom with the other tourists. Dinner would be served family style to all of the guests. It was a thrill to meet people from different parts of the country, and this experience sparked what would be a lifelong fascination of Florida for me.

This trip also revealed the South as it was depicted in books. At a Woolworths store, out of curiosity, I took a drink from the Colored water fountain because I wanted to see if it tasted any different from the White fountain, but I was abruptly pulled away. Restaurants, when they allowed blacks as patrons, had a separate back entrance.

Grandma and Grandpa lived in a little house on a lake just outside of Groveland. Our families would stay in cottages at a Lutheran camp adjacent to his property. Uncle Bob or Uncle Al brought a 25-horsepower motor boat down to the property, and we had loads of fun skiing on the lake.

We'd take the dirt road to town, and a two-track road led to the orchard. The trucks that were used to haul the fruit were impressive to a young boy. After witnessing racism in our travels, I watched with curiosity as Grandpa treated the migrant families

42

with respect, and noticed that it was reciprocated.

In 1959 my dad bought a new car and our entire family drove to the orange grove. The rest of the extended family made the same trip so that we could be together. This time I took my 22-gauge rifle.

After watching me practice shooting, Uncle Bob praised my marksmanship, which meant a lot to me since Uncle Bob had been a bomber pilot in World War II.

One day there happened to be a couple of coots (water birds that look like ducks) in the middle of the lake. Uncle Bob sighted in on one of them and shot it, and all the boys jumped up and down, thinking it was so cool. Bob's wife, Connie, went absolutely nuts and read him the riot act. I had never seen a guy dressed down by his wife like that. Aunt Connie insisted that Uncle Bob, instead of taking the power boat, row out to the middle of the lake and pick up that coot so we could give it a proper burial. Uncle Bob rowed it in and dug a hole to follow his wife's instructions.

We all stood around the grave respectfully, and Uncle Bob spoke some words that have remained in immortality in the minds of the young, impressionable boys in attendance.

To the angst of Aunt Connie and the girls, he had named the coot Donald Duck. Uncle Bob cleared his throat and began his eulogy. "Here lies Donald Duck. He would have lived, if only he'd ducked."

With those words, Uncle Bob became a hero to us, but Aunt Connie went off on him again. This time our laughter drowned out Aunt Connie's reprimands.

Earning my keep at the orchard.

Back at home, our summer days were unstructured. We had very strict rules from 8:00 p.m. (when the street light came on) until bedtime, but just about anything flew during the day. The army of neighborhood kids played from dawn to dusk. My sisters were best friends, only sixteen months apart, and were also surrounded by many neighborhood friends.

I didn't have enough appreciation for my sisters when we were under the same roof. To me, it seemed that they were just in the way. I was a tease and they were my foils. They didn't want to do what I wanted to do, and the more time I spent with them, the more I got myself into trouble, so the smartest approach was to stay away from home as much as possible. (My sisters tell me that they have few childhood recollections of me, and that's simply because I was never home.)

Sharon was an athlete when it wasn't cool for girls to be interested in sports. In her I had an excellent partner in playing catch; she could wing that ball better than many of my friends. She continued to succeed in sports in middle school and high school at a time when there were few opportunities for girls.

I don't remember too much about Donna, but her soft heart was evident from the beginning. Occasionally she brought home stray cats when she could not bear to see them without a home. We had a dog named Smokey, but the dog didn't behave very well and we didn't do a great job cleaning up after it. One day Smokey just disappeared; my dad had given him to a farmer who needed a dog.

Since I wasn't a very nice big brother, I was a handful for my mom.

A Growing Family

The words from her that I most dreaded were, "Wait till your father gets home," because I knew there would be trouble, and there was trouble most nights.

During one summer when I was about ten years old, one of my friends was out of town and I often complained of having nothing to do. I must have been making life miserable for my sisters and my mom.

My dad's advice to me to combat boredom was to dig a hole, which was an exercise that had kept him occupied during his time in the army. I used my dad's WWII army shovel, which had a green handle and a foldable arm that could be locked into position.

I dug the outline of a hole, and after carefully setting aside the sod, I began to dig. I dug, and I dug. The hole became the challenge, giving me something to look forward to every day.

Eventually I dug so deep that I passed a water pipeline. By this time one of my friends asked if he could help. One person would dig, and the other would go up and down the ladder to empty the buckets of dirt. Our huge mound of dirt next to the hole grew every day.

My sister Donna was also intrigued by my new hobby and asked if she could inspect the hole. Although our policy was "No girls allowed," we acquiesced. But when we watched her climb down the hole, a great opportunity arose that we were powerless to resist.

As soon as Donna entered the depths of the hole we took away the ladder. So it turned out that digging the hole did not keep me out of trouble, it just provided an opportunity for more. This resulted in another whooping for me when my dad came home. (My sister has since graciously forgiven me.)

The homes on our street were about fifteen feet apart, and the neighborhood was an interesting melting pot of Dutch, Latvian, Lithuanian, and Polish families. We could call out the surnames of all the families on our block: Nichols, Crapsey, Bazan, Koppenol, Lucas and Cegelis. I don't remember doors being locked, and I can't recall hearing about anything being stolen.

Remarkably, I don't remember seeing a "For Sale" sign in front of anyone's house. It was a neighborhood as I think neighborhoods were represented in television shows like *Leave It To Beaver* or *Father Knows Best*.

There was a firm division along gender lines when it came to our assigned chores. As a boy, my chores were mostly outdoor activities. I was in charge of taking out the trash and washing out the barrel after it was picked up. I'd burn the garbage that wasn't taken.

Our basement had a huge coal furnace, and one room was designated as the coal bin. Every cold night I'd shovel coal from the coal bin to the coal hopper, and in the morning I took the clinkers out of the furnace and put them into the ash can. Mr. Hans, the ash man, would unload the clinkers once a week. My sisters' jobs were all in the domestic category: washing dishes, vacuuming, and the like.

One maxim in our family that I learned very early was that you don't buy it unless you have cash. My dad instilled in me an ethic of exchange and barter. If you don't have the cash, you wait until you do. He was the Dave Ramsey of his time. Dad never bought anything on credit, and nothing was billed. If I needed a new baseball mitt, he'd ask me how long it would take for me to earn it. If I needed a bat, I knew it would be mine after I mowed ten lawns. Needs such as clothing were supplied, but I bought anything extra with money I earned from odd jobs.

A Growing Family

Mowing six lawns every week in the summer with a push mower garnered about fifty cents per yard. We also painted, had paper routes, laid sod, peddled handbills and supplemented with occasional lemonade stands.

Hawking lemonade with Billy Duthler.

Perhaps it was in my bloodlines from Grandpa DeVries (the fruit and vegetables huckster) or from Grandpa Rodenhouse (with his orange grove in Florida and fruit trees in his back yard), but something attracted me to fruit, and my friends and I always found ways to get it.

We built a tree house at the top of the twenty-five-foot-tall pear tree in Billy Duthler's backyard. Slats of wood nailed to the trunk allowed us to climb to the top, where we could watch the world of the west side go by as we ate pears from the tree, often before they were ripe.

Billy lived next door to Mrs. Vermaire, our friend John Koetsier's grandma. Mrs. Vermaire had a big cherry tree in her backyard, which we would climb to gorge on the cherries when they showed the first signs of ripening. Her eyesight was failing, but one day when she heard the ruckus in the tree she hollered, "You boys, get out of my cherry tree! I can hear you!"

I responded, "It's the wind."

Mrs. Vermaire called our parents in short order. They failed to see the humor, and we were sent to apologize. Thereafter, we were very quiet when we visited her backyard.

Uncle Bob had a blueberry field in Fruitport. When the berries were ripe, migrant workers from the south filled most of his needs, but he always had room for more pickers. He'd park his 1955 Ford woody station wagon on the corner of Tamarack and Leonard, and it would soon fill up with my friends and cousins.

On the thirty-five mile trip to the field, Uncle Bob would regale us with stories and make up names for people that we would see on a regular basis, one of whom was a WWII vet who lived in a home bordering the highway. This man had lost his legs in the war and would sit outside the front door, watching traffic. Uncle Bob named him Legless Leo. We would honk and wave at him every morning on the way to work and in the evening as we returned home.

Once in the field, we picked berries and got filthy dirty. When we filled our buckets we took the long walk down a dusty road to bring our berries to the shed. The best place for blueberry wars was in "The Jungle," an overgrown patch rumored to be haunted, with berries twice the normal size and bushes that were big enough to climb.

An outhouse was equipped with catalog pages for toilet paper, and water was procured from pumps that needed lots of priming. A hard day of picking usually produced about twenty pounds of berries for which we were paid six cents a pound. This amounted to a weekly paycheck of $6.00. Uncle Bob would stop on the way home and buy us each a soft serve ice cream cone. My dad wasn't happy with our wages or the state of our filthy clothes, but my mom smiled to herself since she had us out of the house for the entire day. We should have paid Uncle Bob for all the fun we had.

Grapes were the last fruit crop of the summer. Mt. Mercy, a convent that doubled as a Catholic girls' school, had a wonderful grape arbor; the fruits of the vines were used, we thought, for wine. Whatever the use, the grapes were the best we'd ever tasted. Perhaps they were so good because it took so much work to get them.

The "nunnery" arbor was up the steep hill from Raps Woods, just west of Valley Field, where we hiked and shot our BB guns. We scouted out the area and made a path from the top of the hill through a field to the boundary of the outbuildings, then quietly crawled into the area where the grapes were growing. Our idea of quiet roused the nuns, and we fled with them in hot pursuit, their habits hiked up for faster running. We made it to the top of the hill and tumbled down to the bottom...without any grapes.

A plan was hatched. We retrieved large pieces of cardboard from Zoet Hardware and cut them into three-foot squares. We again climbed the hill to check if the cardboard would aid in sliding down the hill for our escape. The trial run was a success. We deposited the cardboard at the top of the hill and snuck down the path to the vineyard and filled a bag with grapes.

When the nuns heard us the chase began! We ran up the path, just ahead of the pursuing nuns, jumped on the cardboard, and slid down the hill to safety.

We ran across Valley Street through a hole in the fence behind Valley Field, and made our way to the first base dugout where we gorged our delicious bounty. Thinking back, we didn't make much of a dent in the grape supply and must have created a whole lot of fun for the nuns. This was repeated for a few years until we became interested in girls and cars.

Once in a while my mom would give me a pile of S&H green stamps. These stamps were given to customers at grocery stores, laundromats, gas stations, etc. The amount of stamps you received depended on how much cash you spent at these establishments, so it was a very popular promotional campaign in the 1950s and 1960s.

My job was to lick the green stamps and arrange them in designated places in a booklet. When the books were filled I could redeem them for anything my heart desired. My first 22-gauge gun was procured by redeeming five books of stamps.

I was the first kid in the neighborhood to buy a BB gun. I had saved and saved for the whole summer, earning extra money by washing the few cars in the neighborhood and picking up paper routes. A store not far from where we lived, Zoet Hardware, was run by my friend Billy Joe Demoray's dad and grandpa. One day I noticed a sign in the window advertising a sale on Red Ryder guns. The sale price was posted in big numbers: $9.95. I knew that my dream would soon become a reality. I counted my coins over and over again, and when I finally reached $9.95, I walked to the store with my pockets full of coins. After I proudly poured the money onto the counter, Mr. Demoray let me inspect all of the BB guns, even though they were all the same.

A Growing Family

After I made my selection he counted the money and said, "This is only $9.95. It's $9.95 *plus tax*."

I'm sure he could tell by the disappointed look on my face that I was not a happy little boy. "Just a minute," he said. He took the gun to the back, wrapped it up in paper and gave it to me.

I went home and tore off the wrappings and cardboard, only to find that, although the gun was there, there were no BBs or targets. Mr. Demoray had removed these extras because I did not have enough money to cover the tax. I learned a very hard lesson that day, and ever since then I have not been a proponent of taxes.

My first bike: a 3-speed Schwinn Stingray.

The combination of owning both a bike and a BB gun was my first taste of freedom.

My friends and I would hike down Walker Road and head west along Indian Mill Creek. One of the kids, Eddie DeKam, had picked up the habit of smoking. The rest of us had no money to buy cigarettes, so we instituted a system. We took a bunch of Hills Brothers metal coffee cans, punched a hole on each side, and ran a wire through the holes. These we would hang from a belt loop.

Half of us would walk along one side of Walker Road and the rest took the other side, and we'd collect cigarette butts that had been thrown from car windows. Then we'd enjoy our spoils. We sat under the Indian Mill Creek bridge and smoked until we got sick. Those experiences may have had the effect of curing us from that particular vice. I don't think anyone from our group (except for Eddie) continued to smoke.

Sometimes our destination was Bending Elm, a beaten path a couple of miles farther. We'd split up on both sides of the creek, and the BB gun fights would begin. One rule was that we could not shoot each other above the waist, and since we were all pretty good shots the rule was not often violated. If another player crossed over to your side, they were fair game. The creek itself was neutral territory. One day John Miedema fell in the creek, and in an attempt to dry his pants he reclined on a tree trunk that had fallen over the creek, making an extremely inviting target. We were powerless to resist, but John did not sustain injury. Despite lack of supervision and untamed spirits, we escaped combat with only minor scrapes and bruises.

For lunch we built a fire and roasted hot dogs on sticks over a fire. Our side dishes were potatoes and apples, which we wrapped in tin foil to bake in the fire. If we arrived home before the streetlights came on, no questions were asked.

For a change of pace we'd bike to the gravel pits, an area that is now Millennium Park. The huge lakes were inviting but unpredictable; some areas were deep, but where there was clay, it was very shallow. Still, we dared one another to climb on the crane booms and dive off.

Hunting and fishing were also favorite activities. Eddie DeKam's dad would take us in his '57 Ford to our makeshift campground where the Rogue

A Growing Family

River flows into the Grand River. By constructing a dragline over the Rogue River we fished for trout.

Meanwhile we shot frogs, and after skinning them, we'd skewer them on sticks and roast them over the fire along with the catch of the day. Corn that ripened in August completed the meal. Eddie's dad would check on us in the evening and ask if we were ready to come back, but usually we'd stay overnight. Our fathers' WWII paraphernalia came in handy. We'd load our supplies in their knapsacks and made good use of their helmets, canteens and mess kits. At night we'd set up their button-closure canvas army tents.

At home we scoured the sports section of the *Grand Rapids Press* and were glued to the radio for sporting events like the Indianapolis 500 and Detroit Tiger baseball. When the Indy 500 was going on, we had simulations with our bikes. The courses wove around the blocks of our neighborhood, and one person, typically someone's sister, would be a lap counter. In designated pit stops, contestants pulled in for orange juice.

"The Cheetah" riggimajig: Billy Duthler, ADV, Jim Eldersveld, and Mark Rickers.

We were inspired to build our own vehicles, which we called "riggimajigs." The bodies were made of plywood and the wheels came from old baby buggies. They featured a split axle with a steering assembly on the floor. Although they looked hot, they were destined to race no farther than the neighborhood alley. Each required a driver and a pusher, whose job was to propel the vehicle with a broom handle. I named mine "The Greyhound," but it only won when the pusher could outrun the others.

Everyone had favorite baseball players and we memorized the stats. Our Cadet group took the train to Detroit in 1959 to watch the Tigers play the Boston Red Sox. Our seats were in left field, and it was the thrill of a lifetime to be directly behind Ted Williams.

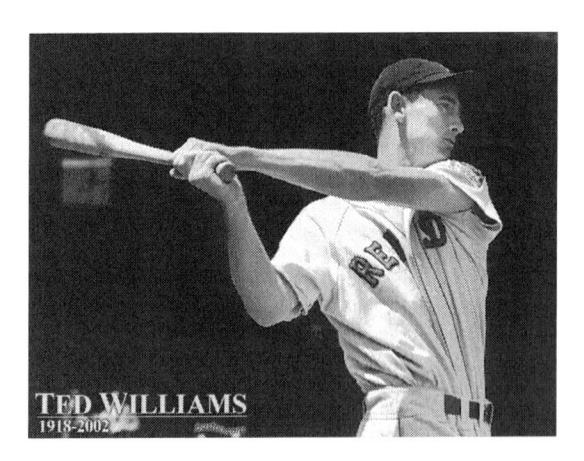

Having no opportunity to play organized ball probably forced me to be the organizer of neighborhood games. The alley between homes was dirty and grungy, not much wider than forty feet, so when we played baseball, modifications were necessary. Instead of a using a standard baseball, we wrapped a plastic practice golf ball in black electrical tape.

For a bat we'd cut the handle from a broom (nabbed from someone's garage), drill a hole in one end, and put a strap of rope through the hole. The batter would put a hand through the strap to ensure that the bat wouldn't go flying after the swing. Only those who were able to earn money had a mitt.

A Growing Family

Even without regulation equipment, we were always able to scrounge up more than enough players for a game.

We all became pretty good hitters, but we learned to drive the ball up the middle over the pitcher's head, because if we went left or right the ball would end up in Mr. Shultz's or Mr. Rickson's yard, and the game would effectively be over.

Grand Rapids has quite a history in baseball. Guys like Willie Horton and Mickey Stanley played on semi-pro teams at Valley Field. Stanley was signed in July 1960 by local Tigers scout Bob Sullivan (of Sullivan's Carpet) for a $10,000 bonus. He played outfield on Sullivan's National Baseball Congress team, which won the national championship in Wichita, Kansas. Stanley would eventually move up to play for the Detroit Tigers.

Once we were able to see Satchell Paige, a legendary pitcher in what was known as the Negro Leagues. His team was the Kansas City Monarchs, and when they played at Valley Field the fans were wall-to-wall and the excitement in the park was electric. Paige later played in the Major Leagues for the St. Louis Browns, and would ultimately be inducted into the Baseball Hall of Fame.

Common Threads: Passion, Perseverance and Praise

The History of Baseball in Grand Rapids

Until the West Michigan Whitecaps began their inaugural season in 1994, Grand Rapids had been without a professional baseball team for 40 years, since the Grand Rapids Chicks disbanded in 1954. But Grand Rapids has a strong history of baseball as more than 30 professional teams, both men's and women's, and dozens of amateur leagues have called this area home since 1883.

Playing in a variety of leagues, the teams went by such nicknames as Furnituremakers, Rustlers, Gold Bugs, Bissell Sweepers, Bill-Eds, Billberts, Billbobs, Dodger Colts, Chicks, Orphans, Jets and Joshers.

The original professional team in Grand Rapids was organized in late 1882 and played as a charter franchise in the Northwestern League in 1883. The team had no nickname and played home games at Recreation Park on weekdays and at Alger Park on Reeds Lake on weekends.

Many teams came and went in the early 1900s, but with the onset of the Great Depression in the late '20's, professional baseball all but ended in Grand Rapids.

Fans were still able to enjoy semi-pro baseball in the area during the Depression. When the Brooklyn Dodgers barnstormed through Grand Rapids in 1939, they discovered more than 50 teams playing in six city leagues. Because enthusiasm for the game was so high, the Dodgers decided to place a farm team in Grand Rapids for the 1940 season. The Dodger Colts, as the team was called, played at Bigelow Field on South Division until the outbreak of World War II ended their stay.

Toward the end of the war, the Chicks of the All American Girls Professional Baseball League (immortalized in the movie "A League of Their Own") came to Grand Rapids from Milwaukee. The Chicks were popular and played excellent baseball, winning the AAGPBL playoff pennant in 1947 and again in 1953, but were forced to disband when the league folded in 1954.

A Growing Family

1953 Grand Rapids Chicks

Locally-sponsored professional baseball all but disappeared during the 1950s as television brought major league baseball into the home. But local baseball legend Bob Sullivan successfully bucked this trend. His team, the Sullivans, were noted for their success in amateur baseball play and in sending players to the majors for almost four decades.

Another local hero, Ted Rasberry, owned the Grand Rapids Black Sox and later the Detroit Stars and the Kansas City Monarchs of the Negro Leagues. Rasberry fought to keep black baseball alive until 1960, when the league, which at one point consisted of 16 teams, shrunk to only four due to the falling of the racial barrier.

The West Michigan Whitecaps are keeping baseball traditions alive. They recognized the rich history of baseball in Grand Rapids with six "Turn Back The Clock" tribute games in 1996. Players dressed in old-time uniforms and played one game each as the 1899 Furnituremakers, the 1903 Orphans, the 1921 Joshers, the 1922 Billbobs, the 1948 Black Sox and the 1950 Jets. Despite the number of teams that have called Grand Rapids home, the Whitecaps became Grand Rapids' first professional sports team to win a championship in 1996. They won the Midwest League championship again in 1998, 2004, 2006 and 2007.[6]

A plum job for me was working as a bat boy for the amateur Sullivans team. However, one stint brought great pain and suffering.

Mr. Sullivan asked if I would be available to work the upcoming Sunday game. Although our Sunday rules precluded this, I told him to count me in. As soon as the family went down for their afternoon naps I made my escape. The ticket taker at the door did not believe my claim to be a bat boy, so I did what my friends and I often resorted to when the gates were locked: I scaled the fence. Since I was wearing my Sunday shoes instead of my tennis shoes, I had trouble climbing the hurricane wire fence and even more trouble when I attempted to jump over the protective barbed wire. My Sunday shirt was in tatters, and my stomach did not look much better. After I ran home my sisters poured mercurochrome on my wounds, and we burned the shirt. I fully believed that God was directly punishing me for my disobedience and lack of judgment.

The Valley fields were in mint condition, so when we had the opportunity we'd ride our **fat-wheeled** bikes and play at the field before the city league games began. We'd hook our mitt over the handle of our bat, lay the bat across our handlebars, and ride to the hardware store to chip in for a ball. When that one turned to mush we chipped in for a replacement.

Since mitts were in short supply, when teams rotated from fielding to batting, we'd drop our mitts at our field positions for the opposing team's use. The junkiest mitt was used for home plate. When city workers kicked us off the diamond we'd make our own field in the center field area.

As if that were not enough, every night after supper we played more ball at West Side Christian School, near the corner of Pine and Leonard. Since this group was typically smaller, the rules were modified. Fielding positions were limited; we had a pitcher, a short stop, a 3rd baseman, and a left fielder. Often it was 3 on 3, and we played without a first baseman.

If the ball was fielded and thrown to the pitcher before the runner reached first base, he was out. If you hit to the right side of second base, it

A Growing Family

was an automatic out. If you hit the building on the fly, it was a home run.

On other summer nights everybody came to our house. My dad was involved with Camp Roger, and my sisters and I would stay at the camp for a week at a time. We took the games back home with us and taught them to our friends: Capture the Flag, Seven Steps Around the House, Kick the Can, and Red Light Green Light.

One night Larry Visser invited a few kids to his house for a sleepover. That night was the advent of my lifelong fear of snakes. We watched a movie on Larry's television with his dad, and the snakes and alligators on the screen scared the bejeezus out of me. When I later glimpsed a snake in Pickerel Lake at Camp Roger I probably did not impress my fellow campers when I latched onto another boy.

Since the only television in close proximity was at Billy Joe Demoray's house, we hardly ever watched TV. My parents both loved the written word and pushed reading. In the hot days of summer my mom made me ride my bike weekly to the library. I loved books that featured sports figures, such as Chip Hilton and Bronc Burnett, and the sense of adventure in the **Hardy Boys** series. After I'd exhausted these, the librarian suggested mysteries, science fiction, history and biographies.

Without the benefit of pictures I'd close my eyes and imagine the adventures of Davy Crockett, Abraham Lincoln, Calamity Jane, and Wild Bill Hickok. Reading these books opened up new worlds, and I pretended to be these characters during frequent BB gun fights.

Ours was the only cement double driveway that was wide enough to accommodate a basketball hoop. In the back of our house was a garage that looked like a small barn with a hayloft at the top. My dad nailed the door of the loft shut, and this became our backboard. The rim did not have hooks, so we'd tape the net to it. We went through nets like there was no tomorrow. When one was ruined we chipped in and ran to the hardware store for a replacement.

In the fall we played football at Richmond Park. If we had a lot of guys we'd each contribute a quarter. The last guy to arrive would take the quarters to the corner market and buy a gallon or two of cider. At halftime we'd pass the jug around until it was drained. To earn money we raked leaves, but the best money to be made was from shoveling snow in the winter.

It seemed to snow a lot more in those days than it does now. The snowplows would bury the driveway entrances, so we had to clear a path for the cars. One of my regulars was the Nichols family on the corner lot. After completing the job, I'd knock on the door. Mrs. Nichols would say, "It looked like you were working hard, so it must have been heavy snow," and she'd give me a dollar. If it wasn't heavy, she'd give me a quarter. On real heavy days we'd put our shovels on our shoulders, knock on doors for extra work, and at the end of the day our pockets were filled with quarters.

We worked a lot, but we played constantly. In the winter we built snow forts and had snowball fights every possible day. The Richmond Park pond was a convenient location for winter adventures. With the knowledge that there was a pretty good chance that our shoes would be stolen, we'd walk to the park on our ice skates, a mile and a half away, to play hockey.

The sledding hill at the park was legendary. On Saturdays we'd arrive early and stay the day. To impress the girls we'd put on our ice skates, crouch down and go screaming down the hill. If you could keep your balance, it was possible to land on the pond at the bottom of the hill and coast all the way across.

Along with a sense of adventure came great immaturity. In those days the plows were not out in the force they are today, and they didn't use salt or sand. Snow tires did not exist; instead, people put chains on their tires. After a good snow, the streets would be slippery when the snow was packed down. My friends and I would sit in the bushes behind Jim Byl's barbershop, at the corner of Tamarack and Leonard. When cars waited at the red light we'd sneak up, grab the back bumper, and squat like baseball catchers. When the light turned green the driver would head north on Tamarack, oblivious to the fact that he had two or three kids hanging onto his bumper. To heighten the danger and fun of what we termed "car hopping," we did this on ice skates.

A lot of our pranks seemed funny at the time, but in retrospect we were very foolish and caused harm to some people. We planted stone-embedded snowmen in the middle of the road and howled with laughter when a car made impact. We strung gasoline-doused rope across the road in the middle of the night, and when cars approached we'd ignite the rope, causing the street to light up. Cars would screech to a halt and bottom out on the cement. We'd do anything to get people to chase us.

As was the case in many Dutch CRC homes, certain activities were "verboten" (i.e. forbidden). My parents didn't approve of television (but finally purchased one for limited use when I was in tenth grade), dancing, playing cards or seeing movies in the theater. Nevertheless, my friends and I regularly attended the triple feature at Our Theater on Leonard and Alpine. We were so afraid of getting caught that we'd post lookouts and run like crazy to get inside without being seen. Saturday matinees were a quarter for a triple feature: first was a horror film featuring Abbott and Costello, then a Captain Easy war film, and finally a western, typically featuring Hopalong Cassidy or Roy Rogers.

One historical event that stands out in my mind was the Soviet Union's launch of the Sputnik and the ensuing space race. I clearly remember the thrill of Billy Joe Demoray's birthday treat that year. When a student brought a birthday treat to school we would all lay our heads on our desks while the birthday kid put a treat in front of us. At the signal we'd raise our heads, sing "Happy Birthday," and enjoy the treat, usually a candy bar.

Billy Joe's treat in 5th grade trumped everybody else's: resting at the top of an uncapped bottle of Dr. Pepper was an aqua-colored gumball covered with sugar crystals that was supposed to resemble the Sputnik. Other companies capitalized on the event and churned out Sputnik merchandise as well.

A Growing Family

The Sputnik got people talking. People were afraid of the existence of a foreign object, this satellite, floating around in space. I remember looking up at objects in the sky from time to time, wondering if I was seeing the Sputnik.

The Brondsmas lived down the street from us, and one day we noticed a couple of guys digging, so we went to investigate. It turned out that they were digging a bomb shelter. All of a sudden the Brondsmas were the most popular family in the neighborhood because if the Russians were going to bomb us, we wanted to be in their shelter. It was big enough for eight people, and everyone kind of visualized where their spot would be when the big one dropped.

Our fear was compounded in school with "Duck and Cover" drills to prepare for the chance attack of a bomb. We were to lie facedown under our desks, which may not have made much sense, but when you're in 5th grade you do what the teacher tells you to do.

The History of the Space Race

History changed on October 4, 1957, when the Soviet Union successfully launched Sputnik I. The world's first artificial satellite was about the size of a beach ball, weighed only 183.9 pounds, and took about 98 minutes to orbit the Earth on its elliptical path. That launch ushered in new political, military, technological, and scientific developments. While the Sputnik launch was a single event, it marked the start of the space age and the U.S.-U.S.S.R space race.

The International Council of Scientific Unions decided to establish July 1, 1957, to December 31, 1958, as the International Geophysical Year (IGY) because scientists knew that this would be the high point of cycles of solar activity.

In July 1955 the White House announced plans to launch a satellite for the IGY and solicited proposals from various Government research agencies. In September 1955, the Naval Research Laboratory's Vanguard proposal was chosen to represent the U.S.

63

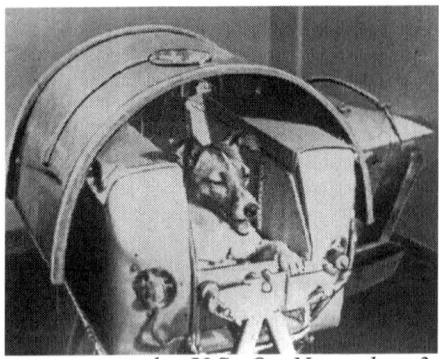

Common Threads: Passion, Perseverance and Praise

The Sputnik launch changed everything. As a technical achievement, Sputnik caught the world's attention and the American public off-guard. Its size was more impressive than Vanguard's intended 3.5-pound payload. In addition, the public feared that the Soviets' ability to launch satellites translated into the capability to launch ballistic missiles that could carry nuclear weapons to the U.S. On November 3, Sputnik II was launched, carrying a much heavier payload, including a dog named Laika.

Immediately after the Sputnik I launch, the U.S. Defense Department responded to the political furor by approving another U.S. satellite project. As a simultaneous alternative to Vanguard, Wernher von Braun and his Army Redstone Arsenal team began work on the Explorer project.

On January 31, 1958, the tide changed when the United States successfully launched Explorer I.

This satellite carried a small scientific payload that eventually discovered the magnetic radiation belts around the Earth, named after principal investigator James Van Allen.

The Sputnik launch also led directly to the creation of National Aeronautics and Space Administration (NASA). In July 1958, Congress passed the National Aeronautics and Space Act, which created NASA.[7]

64

Besides thinking more about global issues at this time, I also learned lessons of mortality. When I was twelve years old I came upon Grandpa DeVries collapsed in the driveway after suffering a stroke. From that time forward his working days were over, and he spent most of his time sitting in his chair.

Some days when I came home from school my parents would ask me to sit with Grandpa so that Grandma could be relieved to do her shopping. Even at that point, they still did not own a car. Grandma was a champion walker and would stroll downtown, pulling her cart that held her purchases behind her.

By this time I had more of an appreciation for my grandparents' presence in my life. They were prayer warriors. Grandpa was a strong, silent presence and Grandma was the glue that kept the family together. Because they lost so many kids and never really got on their feet financially, I believe that they knew what was most important in life. Grandma and Grandpa DeVries were plain people but they loved Jesus, read their Bibles constantly and possessed a strong desire to invest in family.

When it came to money we learned that some had and some had not, but we also knew that even if you didn't have lots of money you could still have a remarkable amount of love. I learned that joy is not found in wealth.

For as poor as Grandma and Grandpa DeVries were, it's ironic that I got the impression that they were rich. I suppose this was because they were so generous. If Grandma had one dollar, she'd find a way to give you two. If I mowed her lawn she made sure that I was paid, even if it was a quarter or a couple of dimes.

My cousin John and I would go to Grandma's every other Wednesday for lunch. She would make paper-thin Dutch pancakes, topped with her homemade raspberry jam, and she got such pleasure in watching how many we could put down. We'd have contests, and the numbers would reach the twenties and sometimes even the thirties.

My grandmother spoke my love language and constantly gave me words of affirmation, convincing me that I was smart and capable of anything when I did not hear those words elsewhere. When I needed to feel loved, I went to her. I began to tune my father out and tuned my grandma in.

Looking back, I wonder if my mom was frustrated because she could not advance in her career of nursing. She had been a competent nurse, and after she became a mother she refused many offers to work with various doctors.

Mom's classic retort when we got hurt was "nature will heal." She'd put mercurochrome on our cuts and send us on our way to tough it out. At the time I thought it was insensitive, but now I see it to be a great lesson. It probably gave me a high tolerance for pain. Mom taught us that we shouldn't sweat the small stuff, and that we needed to take care of ourselves.

I hardly saw my father during these years, as his job was very demanding. Periodically he would travel to the Appalachian Mountains in Kentucky and Tennessee to buy coal anthracite, which would later arrive on the railroad. The engineers would uncouple the coal cars, which would tie up Leonard Street temporarily. Dad and Uncle Bud shoveled coal from the cars onto conveyor belts that led to the coal yard. As soon as one was emptied they would move it down the tracks using something that looked like a long crowbar.

When customers ordered coal for fuel, Dad and Uncle Bud would load their delivery trucks and shovel the coal into basements of homes and businesses. They had no reprieve from the endless soot, and they were always cold since people only needed coal in the winter. This business came to an end when natural gas replaced coal as a means of heating homes.

A Growing Family

The History of Anthracite Coal

The story of anthracite is complex, encompassing not only the pioneering, entrepreneurial spirit of early capitalism and masterful technological and engineering feats, but also the difficult lives of the men and boys who mined and loaded millions of tons of coal and the women and girls who helped hold the mining communities together. Their hard, dangerous, and usually low-paid work brought anthracite out of the earth and into the cities to fuel historic transformations in manufacturing, transportation and market integration.

The Industrial Revolution was well underway in Europe when, according to folk legend, a hunter in Carbon County, Pennsylvania, stumbled across "the black stones." Anthracite was not only harder and denser than the more familiar types of soft coal, but also more difficult to ignite. Once lit, however, anthracite proved to burn longer and more efficiently than its cousins, which turned anthracite into the premier fuel source of nineteenth and early twentieth-century America.

American industry was in its infancy at the time anthracite was discovered and relied primarily on wood and charcoal as fuel sources. As industrialization progressed, alternative sources of energy were needed; there simply were not enough forests to power the hungry factories. With its high carbon content, anthracite appeared to offer a solution, but digging it up, getting it to market, and making it suitable for commercial and household use all proved to be enormous challenges.

Railroads came to dominate the markets. Coal barons, with thousands of acres under their control, became a railroad cartel and held the anthracite region and its people captive in order to supply cities with anthracite. This led to corresponding revolutions in the fueling of industries and the heating of urban residences, which required an army of miners, laborers, mule drivers and slate pickers to extract and process anthracite from "the black hell."

By the Civil War era, coal was king in the United States. The new and often rough-hewn coal communities that sprouted up during the anthracite boom became rigidly defined places, where elite and often arrogant coal operators built magnificent Victorian mansions while their immigrant laborers lived in overcrowded, company-owned "patch towns." Waves of European families arrived to live and work in these isolated company towns.

Courage, a dose of fatalism and the relief of getting out alive after another workday were feelings that cut across the ethnic and religious differences of those working underground. Too often families and communities mourned for fathers, brothers, and sons crushed in a tunnel collapse or burned to death in an explosion.

The Great Depression of the 1930s hit the region particularly hard, and the primary market for anthracite turned to cheaper fuel alternatives such as electricity, oil and natural gas. With fewer and fewer jobs in the anthracite industry, sons no longer followed their fathers into the mines, businesses closed and communities began to empty.

By the later decades of the twentieth century, the once booming coal region had become economically depressed, slowly coming to terms with the painful deindustrialization process that many Appalachian towns and cities continue to experience. Some former anthracite workers still have not escaped other dangers of the mines; after years of inhaling coal dust, they are debilitated by Black Lung or "miners' asthma."

The anthracite boom was a remarkable, revolutionary saga, mixing economic and technological triumphs with human and environmental tragedies.[8]

A Growing Family

When demand for coal plummeted, Dad and Uncle Bud converted their coal trucks into fuel trucks. A partnership was formed with Shell Oil, and Mol & DeVries Fuel was the resulting company. Fuel oil was used for heating only in homes that did not have access to natural gas, typically in the country, so this venture was short-lived.

Storefront window, 619 Leonard Street.

Teenage Years

"I have never let my schooling interfere with my education." - Mark Twain

My childhood on the west side of Grand Rapids was idyllic. The Grand River was the natural boundary, and I don't remember crossing it very often. To me, the west side *was* Grand Rapids. However, at Grand Rapids Christian High School I experienced quite a culture shock.

I discovered that guys on the other side of the Grand River didn't wear blue jeans, tennis shoes and sweatshirts, and they didn't play ball every day like we did. I'd always considered our family quite wealthy, but in high school I discovered that we were lower-middle class.

I had not previously known any kids whose parents were teachers, doctors, or dentists. My friends' parents were all small businessmen or blue collar workers.

Since my birthday was in March, I missed the cutoff to begin school in September, so I began a new grade every January. Our class was the last to participate in this half-year schedule. The entire senior class contained several hundred students, but our little section was comprised of thirty. We started high school after Christmas, so it was an odd feeling to enter high school mid-year.

No school buses serviced our area, so the choices were to pay a quarter per day for the city bus or ride my bike. I chose the latter whenever possible, as my allowance each week was $2.00. To be on a sports team would have been a dream come true, but teams had already been chosen in the fall.

My mom had purchased what she thought was an adequate wardrobe for an incoming high school freshman boy: a new pair of pants and two shirts. On Monday I'd wear my new pants and one new shirt, on Tuesday I'd switch off with the other new shirt and the same pants, etc., so my wardrobe schedule was pretty predictable. Mom would wash whatever shirt I did not wear that day, and it was a pretty good system. The kid that lockered next to me had a different shirt for every day of the month, and he gave me a lot of grief about wearing the same clothes all the time. My classmates had cars, but my buddies and I had bikes. We walked everywhere and thought nothing of it.

School was not difficult and I don't remember studying, but I wish I'd been encouraged to channel my intellect. Perhaps that would have allowed me to avoid learning by experience instead. My grades improved the few times I stayed with Uncle Bud when my parents went on vacation. He would not allow me to leave the designated homework table until assignments were completed to his satisfaction. In my family the question was, "Have you done your homework?" and when the answer was yes, you were free.

My lack of application caught up with me. I had a basic understanding of things that were drilled in the classroom but not much beyond that.

It was in my freshman year that I began to pay attention to politics. When John F. Kennedy ran against Richard Nixon for the Presidency in 1960, both candidates stumped in Grand Rapids.

Nixon came to town on a slow-moving train, much like the trains that would service my dad's coal yard. In those days we'd watch the trains, even jump on the stairs at the back of the car and ride it for a block or two before jumping off. We'd put pennies on the tracks, and after the train passed we'd retrieve our flattened coins.

The train car on which Nixon rode was festooned with red, white and blue bunting. I put a penny on the track and it was flattened by Nixon's train car.

Kennedy came to town in the back of a newly released Galaxy 500 convertible, which got my attention. My friends and I were automobile aficionados, and we'd walk through dealership lots in September and October when the new models were on display and memorize the features.

Kennedy won the election, due in part to his debating and campaigning skills. There was an uproar in our community; people speculated on the impact of having a Roman Catholic in the White House. Many people, including my dad, thought that the pope would make all of Kennedy's decisions and would operate as the de facto President.

73

My peers continued to be a very significant part of my life, and I had some great friends: John Koetsier, Les Nederveld, Denny Byle, Henry Veenstra, and John Miedema to name a few. We took long walks every Sunday and played sports every other day.

Because she was concerned that I was too focused on sports, my mom was always looking for opportunities that would allow me to expand my horizons. One summer day while I was weeding my dad's makeshift vegetable garden that abutted the wire fence between our yard and the Nichols' property, Mom informed me that she'd decided that I would take elocution lessons. I had never heard that word before and would soon regret that I ever did.

Every Saturday morning I took a bus at 8:45 a.m. for my 10:00 a.m. appointment with Muriel Beebe Smith. She was a short little lady who had been exposed to high society, as was obvious in her mannerisms. I also remember that she kept a hanky in her impressive cleavage.

Most of those who sought Miss Beebe Smith's services aspired to be actors or lawyers. Every week she assigned huge chunks of scripts to memorize. When I recited them for her she would judge my gestures, timing, tone and pace. To make matters worse, a performance was held twice a year at the Ladies' Literary Club. I was the most uninterested person in attendance, and my tutor figured that out right away. She knew I would rather be anywhere else on Saturday mornings as well, and I think she felt sorry for me.

One Saturday she said to me, "Would you like to make some money?" So from then on when I arrived at her home on Saturdays she would call in an order to John Kos Grocery Store, we'd go through a perfunctory reading, and I'd pick up her order. She'd pay me fifty cents for my trouble and give me an extra dime so I could grab a cherry phosphate at Middleton Pharmacy while I waited for the homeward bus.

The money softened the blow a bit, but there was still the dreaded semi-annual performance to endure. Most people recited Shakespeare, but Miss Beebe Smith assigned a comedy to me. The formally dressed audience,

Teenage Years

including my dad, was very kind and gracious in their response, so I kind of got into it and found out that I enjoyed making people laugh.

An exciting period of time was when I discovered music. Previously I had only been exposed to Mitch Miller, Lawrence Welk, and whatever records my dad listened to on the 33 rpm Magnavox hi-fi. I also remember vividly listening to *The Lone Ranger* radio show after supper. We'd have our ears glued to the speaker, so excited to hear the introductory song, "The William Tell Overture."

I saved and saved for a transistor radio so I could listen to rock and roll and was finally able to afford one in 9th grade. I did not realize it at the time, but my new pride and joy was "hot." An acquaintance knew I wanted a radio and asked what I was able to pay. I told him that I had $12.00. He soon produced a radio (without the leather carrying case) for exactly $12.00. When I found out that he had stolen it I felt terrible.

My friends and I clipped the transistor on the fence when we played basketball in the driveway. One evening some girls who passed by asked if we liked Elvis. We'd never heard of him, but we made it our business to learn about him to impress the girls.

I identified with the themes of freedom and adventure and loved the stories of the songs. The transistor introduced me to Top 40 rock and roll. First came the likes of Paul Anka, Frankie Avalon and Bobbie Rydell, then came the early bubblegum pop of the 1960s. The Beach Boys and the Beatles emerged at about the same time; I wanted to be like them and learned the words to all of their songs. Much of my income went toward replacement batteries. I would unsuccessfully try to write the song music for my baritone, but it did not copy well.

When I emulated the Beatles' hairstyles, some people at church thought that I should be disqualified to serve as usher. I received an anonymous letter that said it would be appropriate for me to start wearing a dog collar. A couple of men in the consistory challenged my father, saying that the vice president of council should be able to control his son. My new look caused more friction between my dad and me.

Our parents were strict. When Dad gave an order to take care of something "soon," I interpreted this to mean in a day or two, but he meant for it to be done now. I did not understand his language and he did not appreciate my proclivities.

Grandpa Rodenhouse was ready to retire, so **Dad and Uncle Bud purchased his business. Rodenhouse Door and Window became DeVries Brothers Door and Window. This business** operated from the same location as the coal yard, but now there was quite a bit of unused space behind the building. The extra space was leased to a Native American man by the name of George Staggs, who used it for a demolition business. He had a few beat-up trucks and most of the guys who worked for him did not speak English. Back when the four by four was actually still 4" by 4", he would knock down old houses for a song and salvage the wood. The nails that held these pieces of wood together were square. On Saturdays Mark Rickers and I pulled those nails out of the wood for Mr. Staggs for a dollar an hour.

Although I didn't know much about construction, I worked for my dad briefly as a teenager. On the west side, many homes had porches without windows, and my dad's business added custom windows to many of them. He had put a tremendous amount of time into installing windows on the porch of Mr. Sullivan's home, and my job was to caulk the spaces between the bricks

Teenage Years

and the wood frames. I had never operated a caulk gun, and even after I figured out how to make it work, I wasn't very accurate. The caulk spilled through the cracks onto the bricks and the screen, so it wasn't long before Mr. Sullivan sent me home. I soon found steadier work at Meijers, bagging groceries.

When my friends and I turned sixteen, getting a car wasn't an expectation, but Larry DeFouw had a '53 Chevy. It was nothing but rust, but we all pitched in with makeshift sanders, which amounted to large wooden blocks wrapped with a piece of sandpaper. Then we learned how to apply Bondo. After all that work, I still only dreamed of riding with Larry.

Having no cars meant that we had to be creative when it came to dating. I took my first date, Jan Folkertsma, to the roller rink on a city bus. When we returned to the bus stop, I walked her home. She wore tangerine lipstick, and after that first kiss I ran all the way home, constantly trying to sniff the lingering scent of tangerine that had transferred to my lips. I rushed into the house, and the first thing I did was look in the mirror to see if my face had changed. To my disappointment and shock, no such transformation had occurred.

If anyone could convince their parents to allow them to borrow the family car, the rest of the gang would chip in to furnish the gas and buy the driver's dinner, which was usually at the only McDonald's in town, located at 28th Street and Michael Avenue in Wyoming. That was the unwritten rule of the west side.

One night a friend of mine, Ed Bolt, from the southeast side of town picked me up and took me to a ball game. When he dropped me off at the end of the evening I gave him $2.00, and he asked what it was for. I told him that it was for gas. He looked puzzled and explained that his parents paid for the gas, but I insisted on paying him because that's just what we did.

Two days later I received an envelope in the mail from him that contained $2.00 along with a note on a ripped piece of wide-ruled paper that read: "I felt guilty."

It turned out that he lived "on the other side of the river" near Plymouth and Franklin in a home that looked like a castle for kings and queens compared to anything on the west side. The rule that we followed on our side of the river made no sense to him.

In the fall of my junior year I grudgingly took a typing class. Most of the guys in the class were poor typists, including me. We'd get a head start on timed tests, and although our words-per-minute count was high, our numerous mistakes put us in the negative. On November 22, 1963, in the middle of a typing test, the door was thrown open and another teacher yelled, "The President's been shot! The President's been shot." We were dumbfounded. This was not something that we could understand. It seemed like the sun did not shine for the next three days.

Grandpa DeVries also passed away in 1963. When I helped to undress him I found a $20 bill in his shoe. I think that was his bank account. He was poor, but very proud for not accepting help from anyone.

An enormous crowd attended his funeral to honor him. The procession to the cemetery spanned Leonard Street, the likes of which I had never seen at a funeral.

Grandma Rodenhouse also died when I was about sixteen years old. Like a lot of elderly men, Grandpa had difficulty being alone, and my mom would send me out to sit with him. He soon became remarried to a delightful lady named Margaret. A few people in our family resisted her because they believed that Grandpa had not observed an appropriate period of mourning.

In my senior year something clicked, and I began to enjoy high school. At West Side Christian I had always been first chair baritone in band despite the fact that I could not read music because I could copy the tune and had pretty good tone. I was last chair in high school, but after working through several practices I played as well as the first chair. Concert Band was for better players but the less-talented played in Cadet Band. I suffered through this until

Teenage Years

I discovered girls, which became the catalyst for change.

I had simultaneous crushes on Ginny Daverman and Helen Haeck. We sat in the same seat in three consecutive classes. I would write a note for Ginny, she would add to it and leave it for Helen, who would add a little more, and I would take it up the next day. The girls were in Concert Band and encouraged me to try out, but I said I'd never make it. During study hall I would sit and stare out the window, but they convinced me to join them in the band room to practice. The director came in one day to see who was playing the baritone and said, "DeVries, is that you?"

From that moment I advanced to Concert Band and also joined the Pep Band. This opened new doors, and from that moment I started meeting people and actually enjoyed high school.

After graduation in January 1965, for lack of anything better to do I got a job making hot dogs at Thomasma's Meat Company. The employees were simple folks trying to keep their families together. We all paid dues to belong to the Amalgamated Meat Cutter and Butchers Workmen Union. I was paid $1.05 an hour for a job that I absolutely hated.

Although I had just received my driver's license, I did not have a car. I woke up at 3:00 a.m. and walked down Leonard Street in the winter, the only pedestrian at that hour. From the bitter cold outside I entered the facility, which was in essence a cold, stinky meat locker.

After being processed, the meat was blown into long tubes of intestines and tied off with strings at 6-inch intervals. From there they were hung on racks in the smoker for a day or two. In my job as a shaker, I would take the hot dog racks out of the smokehouse and feed the hot dogs through the shaker, where the strings were shaken off.

The hot dogs were then shot into cellophane, shrink-wrapped, labeled, boxed, and sent to grocery stores all over lower Michigan. We made tens of thousands of wienies every day. I found out that the only differences between kosher, all beef, beef and pork, and economy hot dogs were the label and the price.

Soon I moved up from shaker to skinner, from skinner to packer, and from packer to pricer. After receiving a raise I moved to manufacturing. The one thing that set me apart from the other employees was my high school diploma. One thing that we did have in common was our juvenile behavior. This new assignment opened doors for me to prove my immaturity.

As we added meat into the mixer, a common challenge was, "I bet you don't dare put *that* in there." We determined that meat was meat. This included lips, snouts, ears, and anything smaller than a softball. I often ended up on all fours on the floor, laughing so hard I couldn't breathe, imagining someone eating our concoctions. I did not eat hot dogs for years.

After I finished the shift at 12:30 p.m., I'd go home and sit on the heat register for a half hour to warm up. I knew that band class was held last hour, so I decided to join them, even though I had graduated. I got on the city bus with my horn and either played in the band or hung out at the school paper. It ended up being my most enjoyable semester.

At that time Elvis Presley starred in a lot of movies that took place in Fort Lauderdale, Florida, and my friends Bobby Bouma, Ed Ludwick, and I decided to take a road trip. One of my dad's friends, Ed Goudswaard, had won a contest from Pastoor's Meat Company, the prize being four days and nights at the Cadillac Hotel in Miami. Nobody from the west side went to Florida in those days, so when Mr.

Teenage Years

Goudswaard offered the prize as a gift, we gratefully accepted.

Bobby had saved money for a Corvette from his paper route since he was ten years old. He'd found a wrecked 1964 Corvette and rebuilt it in his senior year. Bobby's dad, who worked at Chris-Craft, was a fiberglass magician and taught Bobby the tricks of his trade. They used parts from other cars so that eventually Bobby's Vette resembled Joseph's coat of many colors, but it was mechanically sound.

Bobby trusted no one to drive his precious machine, so Ed Ludwick rode shotgun and I sat uncomfortably between them on the console all the way to Florida. Freeways did not exist, so it was two-lane roads for 1,500 miles and it only took twenty-four hours to reach the Cadillac Hotel.

Lud, Uncle Norm, Bobby, and ADV in Florida.

Since I looked the oldest, I registered us as Mr. and Mrs. Goudswaard. Even the valet knew we were up to no good when he parked the junky Corvette. The room came with a complimentary bottle of champagne. When it was delivered to our room I opened the door and Bobby and Lud could be heard giggling as they were hiding in the bathroom. Every morning two of us would order a huge breakfast in the dining room while the third person hid in the bathroom. We'd eat part of it, and then the third would rotate from the bathroom and finish it up.

Three very immature seventeen-year-olds grew up fast on that trip. Our plan to sleep on the beach was foiled when we were arrested. As we worked our way back to Michigan we became aware of our precarious cash situation, so we picked fruit from orchards and frequented McDonalds franchises, which were just popping up. Two burgers, fries, and a Coke put us out forty-nine cents. We returned with empty pockets, but we'd experienced a priceless adventure.

Returning to my dreadful job provided a stark reality check. One day I took my fifteen-minute break outside on the front steps where I could soak up the spring sun.

I heard footsteps so I moved my knees over and I heard someone say, "Andy, do you work here?"

It was my Uncle Bob. He asked me if I liked what I was doing and when I responded negatively he asked, "Can you drive a truck?"

I lied and said I could, and he asked if I'd like to drive a truck for him. He asked me when I could start.

"Tomorrow," I replied. So I turned in my apron, resigned from the Amalgamated Meat Cutter and Butchers Workmen Union, and became a truck driver for Grand Valley Foods. **That evening I practiced driving a manual transmission until I figured it out.**

Looking back, this seemingly coincidental meeting with Uncle Bob was a providential turning point in my life. **It rescued me from a life of factory work and propelled me toward a more meaningful direction.** Driving a truck may not sound glamorous, but it was wonderful to be released from a miserable job and to experience freedom.

Teenage Years

I delivered Ore Ida shoestring potatoes, sizzle steaks, Gorton's shrimp, Freestone pickles, Mrs. Smith's pies and Suregood shortening to restaurants. When I drove away from the loading dock my time was my own with no one telling me what to do. My work ethic entailed getting things done as quickly as possible, so once I figured out restaurant locations I made good time. My solid rapport with restaurant employees resulted in repeat business and an occasional free hamburger.

The pay was minimal in this job, but the hours were long. I made $1.25 an hour, and when I found out that the other driver, Al, was making $4.00 an hour I was upset. I said to my uncle, "I load Al's truck in the morning, then load mine, make my deliveries and restock the warehouse, then I unload his truck and restock his product and then I finally punch out. That doesn't seem fair."

Uncle Bob said, "Al's married. He has a family of six to support." That made sense for about ten minutes.

Soon after, I noticed that many of my customers were collect on delivery (COD). Uncle Bob was experiencing cash flow problems because many of his customers were slow to pay. The business began laying off employees until just Al and I remained. Two food brokers bought the business, infused some cash and turned it around. One of the men was an absolute godsend. His name was Bill Carlson, and he became my first mentor.

I was having serious problems at home relating with my dad and we argued constantly. I was also starting to date and thought I could set my own hours, which became another source of tension. If my dad said black, I said white. Bill was a wonderful Christian man and a good listener as well as a good boss. He became my surrogate dad. Despite my proclivity for making mistakes, I knew it was safe to bounce ideas off of him. This made working for him a real joy, as he was willing to stay after work to help me understand the complexities of life.

One problem remained: the company didn't pay any differently than Uncle Bob did, and Al was still making all the money but I was doing all the work. I had to leave, so I took a job at Meijers again. A new Thrifty Acres store opened in 1965, and baggers earned a quarter an hour more than Bill was paying.

Pandemonium struck in the parking lot and in the store on opening day. I had never seen so many people shopping in one place. Customers were lined up at every register and the pressure was intense. While I was bagging furiously, someone tapped me on the shoulder to get my attention. I didn't look up but I asked if they needed some help.

"Young man, you need a haircut," came the reply.

I already had a dad at home that gave me constant grief about my hair, so this comment was not appreciated. I informed the voice that he could keep his opinions to himself and he told me to look at him. To my surprise, I found myself looking at Mr. Fred Meijer himself.

I thought to myself, *I don't need this*, and responded to him, "If it's so important to you that your baggers have short hair, perhaps it would be best if you found someone else to bag for you." I took off my apron, punched out and went back to work for Bill. He was thrilled and gave me a raise.

(In years following, I became friends with Fred Meijer and told him that story. He remembered the incident and we shared many a laugh over my impetuous nature.)

At this time I began dating Valerie, a young lady that shared my joy of adventure. As we became more involved, she was making plans for college and informed me that she had second thoughts about being in a relationship with a truck driver. After discussing this with Bill, I had serious thoughts about college. Mom, overjoyed, promised that she would buy me a new Mustang if I graduated from Calvin College.

In the meantime, dating was becoming expensive, so I applied for a Fuller Brush sales route and was hired on commission to sell cleaning products

Teenage Years

door to door on the west side of Grand Rapids. I had so much confidence that I would be successful; unfortunately, that was not the case as I wore out a couple of pairs of shoes walking up and down the sidewalk, knocking on doors with very few sales.

I turned in my sales kit and found a job at a full service gas station. As soon as I finished at Grand Valley Foods, I walked down the street and pumped gas. As credit cards had not been invented, regular customers ran a tab, which they were expected to pay at the end of the month. Recognizing customers and knowing how to spell Polish and Dutch names came in handy. We had the lowest prices in town, and workers literally ran from car to car. Automatic shut-offs had not hit the market so we created our own by sticking a pencil in the pumping mechanism to keep the gas flowing. The trick was to remember where you left the pencil as you rushed from car to car.

One time I misjudged, and to my horror a stream of gasoline from an overfilled gas tank flowed down the street. The fire department cleaned up the mess and it took me a week to pay for the spilled gas.

Later that year Grand Valley Foods was sold to Dykstra Poultry, a leading distributor of fresh and frozen poultry looking to expand into the restaurant business. Al and I were allowed to keep our jobs and were introduced to the Teamsters Union. Now we were paid the same! No longer did I need extra jobs. My wages more than doubled, but the work was much harder and now a foreman told me when and where to jump. *Just what I needed,* I thought. *Another dad.*

As the new guy, I got the tough jobs. Each day we unloaded semi trucks that hauled 500 crates of freshly killed chickens from Alabama and Georgia. This was before semis had refrigerated trailers, so the dead chickens were packed with ice and each crate weighed 100 pounds.

Soon after I paid my dues in this assignment I was given some of the driving jobs. This company had better equipment, bigger trucks and plenty of extra work if you wanted to stay late and help the butchers. A few of the

85

country clubs in town had standing orders for boneless chicken breasts, which required tediously and painstakingly deboning the chicken breasts by hand. But extra work meant more money, and college was looming.

A highlight at this time was that I was able to buy a Triumph motorcycle in 1967, which provided the freedom of a bicycle times ten as my scope and distance increased. My only goals were to make money and have fun.

Independence and Higher Learning

"College is a refuge from hasty judgment."- Robert Frost

Having been away from school for a while, the transition to college was a challenge. Dykstra Poultry allowed me to work as much as I wanted, and I took advantage. Regrettably, I enjoyed work more than school.

I would take the truck to school, attend classes, and then make deliveries. Some Saturdays required the delivery of chicken to one of the Michigan prisons, and I would take my current girlfriend for the ride and identify her as a co-worker.

At this time I was incredibly distanced from my father because of everything from political beliefs to philosophies about goals in life, and I knew I had to get out of the house. It was a contentious time in our lives, and although I regret how it played out, in retrospect it probably needed to happen.

I moved into a rental with friends at 1140 Lake Drive, becoming independent sooner than I'd planned. Being cut off financially necessitated that I become responsible for my own living expenses, transportation costs and tuition, with little money left over for investing. On the upside, some of the best times of my life involved living with these friends. We were like family; we ate every evening meal together and played basketball every chance we could, competing in city recreation leagues. A highlight was when our coach, Bill Carlson, arranged for us to compete against prisoners in state penitentiaries.

One significant historical event that happened during my college years was when Neil Armstrong walked on the moon. Mark Rickers and I joined our friend Bill VanderVelde, recently returned from the army, at his parents' house to watch the coverage on television, Miller Longnecks in hand.

Apollo 11: Man on the Moon

The day that men from Earth first set foot on the moon was the culmination of years of research and development, success and failure, and bitter competition from our feared rivals.

In 1957 Armstrong was selected for the ironically named Man In Space Soonest (MISS) program. Then in September of 1963 he was selected as the first American civilian to fly in space. (Russia launched civilian Valentina Tereshkova into space in June of 1963.)

*Initially, it was planned that **Buzz Aldrin**, the Lunar Module Pilot, would be*

Independence and Higher Learning

the first to set foot on the Moon. However the positions of the astronauts in the module would have required Aldrin to physically crawl over Armstrong to reach the hatch. As such, it was decided that it would be easier for Armstrong to exit the module first.

Apollo 11 touched down on the surface of the Moon on July 20, 1969, at which point Armstrong declared, "Houston, Tranquility Base here. The Eagle has landed." A huge sigh of relief was breathed throughout mission control, as it was thought that Armstrong had merely seconds of fuel remaining before the thrusters cut and the lander plummeted to the surface.

Armstrong and Aldrin exchanged congratulations before quickly preparing the lander to launch off the surface in case of an emergency. On July 20, 1969, Armstrong made his way down the ladder, and as his left boot made contact with the surface he then spoke the words that defined a generation, "That's one small step for man, one giant leap for mankind." Interestingly, he meant to say "one small step for a man," referring to himself. Otherwise the phrase is actually contrary, since as stated, man would imply mankind.

About 15 minutes after exiting the module, Aldrin joined him on the surface and they set to investigating the environment on the lunar surface. They also planted the American flag on the surface. But because of a malfunction of the bottom extender of the flag, the flag appeared to be waving. This, of course, would be impossible since there is no air on the Moon.

The final task carried out by Armstrong was to leave behind a package of memorial items in remembrance of deceased Soviet cosmonauts Yuri Gagarin and Vladimir Komarov, and Apollo 1 astronauts Gus Grissom, Ed White and Roger Chaffee. Armstrong and Aldrin spent 2.5 hours on the lunar surface.

The astronauts then returned to Earth, splashing down in the Pacific Ocean on July 24, 1969. Armstrong was awarded the Presidential Medal of Freedom, the highest honor bestowed upon civilians.[9]

Since I was now independent there was more pressure to stay solvent, which led me to accept even more work, often at the expense of studying. If I had any extra cash after paying for necessities, it went toward concerts. When I saw the Beach Boys live, I thought I was in heaven. Music was now a constant in my life. If I had a date, I'd cram the transistor radio between the dashboard and the front window since the models that I drove were not equipped with built-in radios. (Even today, when I hear a song from long ago I connect it to the girl that I was dating at the time.)

While taking a history class, I knew that I needed to do well on an exam, so I asked the professor for an extension. With little sympathy he informed me that I had all night to study, so I did just that. The radio kept me going, and on my way to the exam I realized that, while I knew all of the words to Bobby Fuller's *"I Fought the Law and the Law Won"* I had not retained the test material.

The movie *Patton* was released at this time, and my dad actually went to see it in the theater. I recently found a piece of paper on which my father had typed, in part,

"I was with the 3rd Division under George S. Patton. As a courier, I was given an assignment to deliver classified information to his headquarters. The plane (which we nicknamed The Maytag Washer) had a load capacity of 365 pounds, so we had to remove our battle helmets to meet the weight restrictions. When I arrived with the attaché case shackled to my wrist, Patton asked, "Where is your helmet?" and without waiting for my explanation he said, "Fine that man $5.00." I never thought I would be so proud of being fined $5.00!! I am also proud to have served under Patton."

This incident was mentioned in the *Patton* movie, although my father's name was not stated. He must have been shocked but pleased to hear the reference; he attended the movie again and again, but he did not talk about it. From that time forward he also lifted the ban on watching movies in the theater.

The Vietnam War had started with the United States sending troops under President Kennedy's watch, but it soon escalated to a full-blown conflict. The more I found out about the war, the more I became opposed to it, almost considering going to Canada, which created more issues with my dad.

If a male college student maintained a 2.0 grade point average he was excused from being drafted. If your grades fell, the draft board was immediately informed of your shortcomings. This was the impetus that forced me to focus on my grades.

I'd ask my professors, "What do I need to do to earn a C?" At a rigorous academic liberal arts school like Calvin, that fell on deaf ears, as most professors felt little sympathy for the plights of those who were not working to their best ability. I changed majors often and took classes just to fill my schedule, rarely meeting with an adviser.

Another distraction that year came in the form of yet another sport. The National AAU Volleyball Championship tournament was played in Calvin's newly constructed Fieldhouse, even before it was utilized for Calvin's own sporting events. People came from all over to watch, and I determined that watching every game was a much higher priority than my coursework. I skipped classes for an entire week and made a decision to seek out opportunities to be involved in this new fascination. Years later I was selected to join the YMCA travel team that had played at Calvin.

Although my timing stunk, I decided to hitchhike to Florida during Christmas break. From this experience I learned things that could never be taught in a classroom. I traveled with moonshiners, coal miners, and truckers whose English was not the same as mine. The longest ride came from two "gentlemen" in a 1964 flamingo-pink Thunderbird convertible. It turned out that, in their "business" dealings, they had exchanged some Polaroid pictures of an older wealthy woman in West Palm Beach (engaged in compromising positions) for this car. They tried to convince me to go into business with them, but I would have no part of it, and we parted ways as soon as we reached the Sunshine State.

My impromptu trip caused me to miss my final exams and resulted in horrid first semester grades. I panicked, knowing that a repeat would put me in a uniform and heading overseas, so I cut back on work and earned better grades the second semester. At the end of the first year, I had poor grades and little idea of what I wanted to do.

Things were going well with Valerie that summer until she transferred to a nursing school in Chicago. I took her mom's car to Chicago on weekends so we could see each other. Although her mom tried to keep me focused on school and on Valerie, neither worked. School, work and playing ball, along with moving in with friends away from home proved to be too much of a distraction, and I barely remained eligible to avoid the draft.

One of my most influential professors at Calvin College, Gordon Spykman, taught religion. He'd had polio, but he didn't let anything slow him down. I had turned my back on the church for a while, but his words intrigued me. I found out that he served as a guest minister, so I followed him from Sunday to Sunday to various churches just to hear him because he was so fascinating.

Professor Spykman's seventy-five-minute-long religion classes were in the middle of the day, so I would buy two Payday candy bars, open them up at the start of class, and lay them side-by-side across the top of my desk. As he lectured I would take notes, simultaneously eating what served as my lunch, picking off one nut at a time.

On a bet, I continued to ride my motorcycle through the winter. This was before electric starters, and one morning I wore out my right leg trying to start my bike. I finally got it started with my left leg, but the drive to campus was bitterly cold. My leather pants creaked as I walked down the hallway to the classroom. My hands were bright red and my fingers were so frozen, it took a while before I could straighten them to take notes. I was asked to stay after class.

Sporting long hair and a beard, I must have appeared rebellious. After

Independence and Higher Learning

class Spykman said, "Andy, I have a son like you. He and I just do not understand each other. I'm hoping that you can help me understand him."

(As providence would have it, thirty-five years later through my job at Calvin, one of the contacts to which I was assigned shared the same last name as this professor. It turned out that he was Professor Spykman's son.)

Although I didn't spend time at home, I was able to connect a bit with my sisters at college. Sharon knew how to make and keep a dollar. She lived at home as a Calvin College student and paid her way as a swim instructor and pool director at the YMCA on Leonard. She commuted on an 80cc, 150-miles-per-gallon Suzuki motor scooter. I enjoyed seeing my unconventional sister buzz around campus.

Donna visited me and baked cakes for special occasions. One year she dropped off my favorite: red velvet cake with white frosting. Four days later she called and said that she'd put a lot of time, money and effort into making the cake, and she did not appreciate the fact that I did not call.

I said, "What cake?"

My roommates first vociferously denied, then sheepishly admitted that they had each tried a bite and then finished off the cake and agreed not to tell me.

Spring Break with Oscar Kleinhuizen in Florida, 1969.

Ron "Oscar" Kleinhuizen and I traveled in 1969 to Florida for spring break in his Volkswagon minibus. Since its top speed was fifty-one miles per hour we usually led a slow caravan of backed-up cars, especially up the mountains. We exchanged our labor for a hotel room, and to pay for meals we hustled basketball like the guys in *White Men Can't Jump*. We defrayed the cost of our rented surfboards by sub-leasing them.

A lovely girl, Joanne Kay Grond, arrived at Calvin from California that year. One night I planned to meet someone at a dance, but when that fell through I looked around for someone else to accompany me. I saw a girl with a short skirt, a great pair of legs and long blonde hair. I approached Kay and asked if she would like to go to the party. We hit it off. She was a California girl, and I kind of thought of myself as a California dreamer.

The next day when one of my friends reminded me that I'd asked Kay out for that evening as well, my roommates and I sat around to hatch a plan. I didn't want to spend a lot of money on a girl I didn't know. One of my friends had been in a wedding the night before and still had the tuxes, and he suggested that we pretend that our house was an underground upscale restaurant called Skipper's.

I went to Woodland Mall to pick up Kay when she finished her shift at a shoe store, and she looked fabulous. We pulled into the driveway, and my friend Norm came out in a tux and said, "Welcome to Skipper's." We got out of the car and I handed Norm the keys.

I played along and said that not many people knew about this great restaurant, but I had connections and was able to make reservations. Kay was impressed that there was valet service on our first date. When we walked in Skip Zwemer approached us in a tux and said, "Welcome to my place. We have the room ready for you."

Jim Kett, ADV, Doug Timmer, Skip Zwemer, Jene Vredevoogd, 1969.

While I was gone my roommates had cleared all of our motorcycles from the formal dining room and replaced them with a big oak dining table covered with a tablecloth and two chairs on opposite ends. Doug Timmer entered in his tuxedo with a Calvin gym towel over his arm said, "Welcome to Skipper's. Would you like to hear the specials?"

We said that we'd already eaten and asked about the dessert specialty.

"Peaches flambé," answered Doug with a deadpan look.

What we had in the house was some really cheap ice milk, and to that my friends added the cheapest yellow cling peaches. They poured brandy over the concoction and lit it in the kitchen. When their laughter erupted, Kay realized it to be the joke that it was, that the whole thing was a scam. Despite these antics, she continued to go out with me.

Soon after we met I stopped at Kay's dorm to give her a ride on my chopper. I lost control on loose gravel when I went too fast into a tight, highly banked curve on Burton Street. My right leg was caught under the bike but my leather jacket saved my upper body.

Kay flew off the bike into a pile of freshly raked weeds, escaping injury. I picked up the bike, persuaded Kay to get back on, and took her home. After checking myself into emergency at Blodgett Hospital, I passed out from shock and blood loss. Surgery was performed to reattach severed ligaments and to suture various cuts.

Kay (on the porch of 1140 Lake Drive) and the chopper, August 1970.

My draft board wanted to see me because my grades were slipping, but this accident bought some time. After a couple months of healing I went downtown to the Federal Building with about 200 other draft-eligible young men. We were assigned to four buses for a trip to Fort Wayne in Detroit. Our bus didn't start, so a substitute bus was dispatched and the first group left without us.

Our bus was filled with antiwar protesters who weren't the least bit interested in supporting this war effort. One of the young men brought a copious amount of weed, which he and his buddies smoked in an effort to jack their blood counts. Another guy with diabetes was willing to share his urine when a sample needed to be taken.

The school bus was so cramped that my already damaged leg became terribly swollen. When we arrived, my pants had to be cut off at the knee so my leg could be examined, and our new best diabetic friend supplied urine in a common cup for about six of us. Another dozen were in dreamland from smoking marijuana, and the doctors were not at all interested in processing us since we had arrived late. My 2-S school designation was turned into a 4-F (physically unable to perform) for a year.

By this time the pressure on the Johnson administration to end the war was intense and the draft situation was deemed unfair, so a national lottery was established for every male over eighteen. Birth dates drawn at random now determined who would enter service. A large group of our friends sat by the television and watched feverishly as our destinies unfolded. Each date was met with excitement or agony. Two friends' numbers were pulled within the first ten drawings. We were so sorry for them, but thrilled for ourselves.

As more dates were called out, I thought I must have missed hearing mine. Three hundred dates had been called, and March 9 had not yet been announced. When my birthdate was finally called as number 317, Kay and I danced and hugged. Four years of uncertainty were over for me but just starting for many of my friends. Some signed up for the National Guard, some joined the Navy, and others dusted off instruments from high school to try out for the Army band. Conscientious objectors made plans to leave for Canada.

A couple of my buddies, Jim Storm and Jack Jolman, died in Vietnam. I read their names many years later on the memorial wall in Washington, D.C. We had played ball together, I'd been in their houses, but they left and never came back. Those were very difficult times.

Despite being on academic probation I was elected for Student Senate and placed on a social events committee. After suffering through concerts by Peter Nero and Ferrante and Teicher, we brought in some big name entertainment. I introduced Kenny Rogers and the First Edition to a sold-out audience. Before the concert I hung out with them backstage and had my first introduction to weed as they prepared for their concert. We later brought in Neil Diamond and comedian Albert Brooks for another sold-out show.

When Spiro Agnew, Nixon's Vice President and a Vietnam War hawk, was to visit Calvin's campus we staged a protest. Another issue that we protested was compulsory daily chapel, which had been in existence since the inception of the college.

A brush with the law led to a brief suspension. All of the guys in our house were seniors except for Skip Zwemer, who was a freshman. In order to avoid the requirement of first-year students living in the dorm, he was registered as Jene Vredevoogd's nephew.

ADV and Skip Zwemer.

Skip came into the possession of four cans of beer, one each for he and his friend and their girlfriends. Rumors of a party at 1140 Lake Drive spread like wildfire, and when Kay and I arrived at the house it was packed with under-aged drinkers. When we noticed three big bald guys in uniform, the effect was like rats leaving a burning ship, but those of us who were twenty-one were hauled to the downtown station. In my one allotted phone call I informed Skip where my money was hidden, and he brought my wad of twenties to the station to bail us out.

The next morning a front-page article in the *Grand Rapids Press* announced that a Calvin professor had hosted a party in which alcohol was supplied to minors. (One of our roommates taught PE as an adjunct professor and coached soccer.) We thought we were free and clear because members of the CRC did not take delivery of the Sunday paper on principle, but the article was repeated the next day to make an address correction.

I did not care about the letter that was sent to our parents, but the $100 fine irked me, so I took a can and circulated the Calvin cafeteria to collect money from the other partygoers to defray the cost. My roommates and I were all suspended for a week, but were able to finish the semester.

Temporarily free from academic concerns, some friends and I discovered a dilapidated cottage on the boardwalk of the Holland Beach. I traced the owner from the name on the beat-up mailbox and made a deal with him. He allowed us to rent the cottage from Memorial Day through Labor Day for $600 as long as we helped with the upkeep. Our nickname for the cottage was the "Cat House," much to the consternation of our girlfriends.

A somewhat friendly rivalry developed over those summers with the park rangers, whose cottage was next to ours. We were too loud and rambunctious for their tastes, and they were authority figures with rules to enforce. But we solved the tension by playing softball with them every weekend. The losers had to buy the beer. The rangers never won a game, and since Ottawa was a dry county, they drove often to Saugatuck.

By this time, close to graduating, I had decided to become a teacher. My grades were too low to apply for student teaching, so in order to improve my grades I took courses that sounded interesting. The study of the mind seemed fascinating, so I gorged my schedule with Psychology classes. After two semesters my GPA was sufficient, and I was assigned to a public high school in Byron Center where anyone with long hair who rode a chopper was considered a hippie.

I was assigned to the greasers and the geeks and made up my mind to connect with them. They showed tremendous interest in my bike, which gave me an idea to teach an after-school class on cycle riding and safety. The local sheriffs department agreed, and a local pastor who also had a passion for motorcycles offered the use of a camp in Tustin, Michigan, that was affiliated with his church.

These boys participated in intramurals for the first time and had a riot. They called themselves the "Green Wienies" and showed up for the first game with three-foot-long green foam hoses hanging from their shorts. I had created a monster, but the boys behaved so well that I was able to take them to the camp, where we rode cycles on trails, fished, built campfires and had a great time.

Dr. Barney Steen, chair of the Calvin PE department, noted something in my performance that had been sadly lacking in previous years: passion. He gave me the only 4.0 that I had ever earned and wrote a tremendous recommendation for me. This turned me in a positive direction, and for the first time I really thought teaching was a calling.

For a last hoorah before finding a real job, Bill VanderVelde and I enjoyed the California surf culture for a couple of weeks that summer. I'd never experienced anything so exhilarating; catching a great wave made me scream for joy.

Finding a teaching job proved to be a challenge. My goal was to be a high school teacher and coach, but I didn't often land interviews and was never asked back for a second one, probably because of my long hair and my penchant for riding a motorcycle. I didn't look like a teacher. I went from an emotional high to a very realistic low. Of the thirty PE majors graduating that year, only two were offered employment. Many of my friends found jobs in other fields.

I had proposed to Kay so the pressure was mounting. Dykstra Poultry provided continued employment, but doing the same job that I had done for five years gnawed at me, so I applied for a substitute teaching position with the Grand Rapids Public Schools. I found steady work in the roughest schools; I may have looked intimidating, and I did not accept any grief from students. It was steady work but still impermanent and did not provide benefits such as insurance.

My dream of teaching and coaching did not look promising, so I widened my exposure and applied for junior high and elementary substituting. With this approach I hit the jackpot. Male elementary teachers were not yet common, but I went for it.

Alexander Hamilton School offered me a long-term subbing assignment in second grade. It was immediately evident that, for the younger students, my height was intimidating, so I determined that the best way to teach them was to be at their eye level. I spent the entire day on a gym scooter board. At 2:30 the principal, Mr. Vercillino, came in the room and saw that I had the kids in the palm of my hand. I realized that maybe high school wasn't right for me.

Mr. Vercillino called me back again and again. He asked me to do a long-term subbing assignment in first grade, and I loved it. Still, getting called at 6:30 every morning made it hard to plan, and my finances were in a shambles so I started officiating basketball, baseball and soccer and took a night job selling snow-covered swampland for a fly-by-night company in

Grand Rapids. School was close to breaking for the summer and I was nowhere nearer a full-time job, so I also took a job driving a truck for Superior Seafoods.

When I heard about an opening at Jenison Christian School I jumped at the opportunity, as did every other Calvin education major. This time I had some experience and a ton of confidence. I borrowed a sport coat, climbed on my chopper and rode to Jenison with high expectations. It appeared that this was an uphill battle since the culture at this school was similar to that of Byron Center. Although the superintendent, Dr. Ken Bootsma, liked me, the school board was unanimous in its dislike for hippies, so I offered my services as a substitute teacher at no charge to Dr. Bootsma, hoping he'd give me a chance, and he responded with a big grin.

Two days later Bootsma called and asked if I would sub for a week in band. I taught with the same gusto that I had taught PE to the "Green Wienies" in Byron Center. The board made me an offer, contingent upon a haircut. A key turning point in my life was when Ken Bootsma had faith in me. He stood up for me to provide what turned out to be an incredible twelve-year career.

In mid-August I headed to California, where I would marry my best friend.

Marriage and Responsibilities

"A journey is like marriage. The certain way to be wrong is to think you control it." - John Steinbeck

My role in planning our wedding was simply to show up. I flew out to California with my best man, Bill VanderVelde. Our guests rolled in, some in a classic hippie van: a Ford Econoline with carpeted walls and floors.

Kay's father, Neal Grond, broached the question of the rehearsal dinner. I had no idea that this was traditionally the responsibility of the groom's family; my parents and I were distant and my own funds were terribly thin. My father-in-law proved himself to be a man of class, and in twenty-four hours he transformed his backyard into a Japanese garden, complete with lanterns from end to end. I supplied the Kentucky Fried Chicken and a case of Coors beer.

My groomsmen and I enjoyed the incredible surf of the Pacific Ocean on the day of the wedding. My best man and I left to get ready for the ceremony, and the rest of the groomsmen vowed to follow.

Kay and I were married on August 21, 1971, in the chapel of the Bethel Reformed Church in Bellflower, California. My groomsmen hitched rides and straggled in, but Ron Kleinhuizen came so late that one of the ushers held his place in front of the church until we threw him into his tux.

My bride walked down the aisle, resplendent in a gorgeous dress (that had cost only $50) and fresh flowers woven into her hair. She looked like a beauty queen to me, and I was choked up with emotion. *Wow, did you get lucky*, I thought. The ring I slipped on her finger was met with some surprise. I'd had no money for an engagement ring and had told Kay that I could only afford a simple wedding band. However, my jeweler friend Mark Fryling convinced me to add two diamonds to the band, which I paid for by officiating ball games for the next month. It was worth it when I saw Kay's reaction when I slipped that ring on her finger.

A predictable ham-buns-and-jello-salad reception was followed by a party at Kay's parents' home. Kay had arranged for us to stay at The Plush

Marriage and Responsibilities

Horse, a hotel in Redondo Beach. We pulled in so late that the office lights were off. When the proprietor finally shuffled in after our repeated knocking, he said that we would not be given our room because of our tardiness. After we explained that it was our wedding night, he begrudgingly showed us to a room but informed us that checkout time was 9:00 a.m. To add insult to injury, the charge for that room soaked up half of my budget.

San Francisco was our intended honeymoon destination and we headed off in a Chevrolet Corvair, one of the earliest high-mileage automobiles. We soon came upon the town of Solvang in which a Danish festival was taking place, complete with giant beer steins, brats and high-kicking frauleins. We purchased a copy of Cannery Row at the John Steinbeck Museum gift shop in Monterey and read the words to each other, tracing the evolution of the book as we traveled the topography that was its setting. On a shoestring budget, we never did make it to San Francisco, and I promised Kay that some day I would give her a real honeymoon.

For the trip home we duct-taped our wedding gifts in a barrel from a dairy farm that had been used to store udder balm. Since we had no money for tickets we waited for standby seats, and when we finally disembarked in Grand Rapids we were down to pocket change.

When Kay and I began our lives as a couple we were as naïve as most newlyweds tend to be. Although I had learned about living in community, I hadn't learned what it meant to be a husband. There was so much that we just made up as we went along.

Among the topics that we hadn't discussed before marriage were finances. My first check from Jenison Christian was $86, which was about half of my truck driver wages. I was so excited to get the teaching job that I hadn't looked at the contract details. Since Kay didn't want to live with my friends, we needed a place to stay, but an additional expenditure was Kay's remaining year of tuition, so we looked for a place where we could work for room and board. Together we managed a thirty-six-unit apartment complex for two years in exchange for rent. Kay cleaned ovens and refrigerators while I operated an industrial carpet cleaner, mowed the lawn, serviced appliances, and shoveled snow. I worked for the tightest tightwad I've ever met, but we did what we needed to do and toughed it out.

Kay drove my temperamental winter beater that had no working heater or windshield wipers, while I rode my cycle. When the snow fell I caught a ride with another teacher for fifty cents a day. To supplement my salary I drove a bus route before and after school, and every noon hour I held a stop sign at the street to direct traffic for kindergarteners for fifty cents a day. Still, we scrambled just to get by, but our friends were also poor. When everyone is broke, everyone is happy.

Music was a priority, and we did manage to purchase a stereo system. My friends and I discovered album-oriented rock before it became mainstream, from Genesis and Pink Floyd to the blues and Motown, and we traveled great distances to hear live music. Along with a couple hundred other fans, we saw the Moody Blues when they performed in a local church.

When I began to teach at Jenison Christian in 1971 the PE equipment room was virtually empty. The PE program had consisted of sharing a ball, standing in line, and watching. My joy was getting all children involved, and it was my mission to figure out ways to create movement. We did a lot with locomotive movement: running, jumping, skipping, etc., but when it came to manipulative motor skills such as throwing, catching, kicking striking, and tumbling, we did not have proper equipment.

Marriage and Responsibilities

As kids started to become excited about PE, those stories went back home. Parents showed their support by participating in the Boxtops for Education program. We all ate a lot of cereal, but our efforts were rewarded. Soon boxes of balls started to appear, and before long every kid in the gym had their own ball.

One thing that surprised me when I began to teach was that so many kids just stood around at recess. This was coffee break time for teachers, but I didn't like coffee, so I joined the kids outside and started a running club. I didn't particularly like to run, but I wanted the kids to do something.

We ran a mile on the first four days of the school week and two miles on Friday. The club grew, and soon a couple hundred kids were running every day. They were featured in a front-page newspaper article.

The kids were motivated to compete, so I lined up buses on Saturdays, and the first sixty kids to show up traveled throughout west Michigan to compete in 5ks and 10ks, which were just beginning to pop up.

Tremendous runners emerged from that club, some achieving All-State and All-American collegiate status. These kids were not big enough for football or tall enough for basketball, but they had found a niche.

One little girl who could barely look me in the eye asked if she could run with me. Because she was slow, I ran with her in a 10k, and when we crossed the finish line everything had already been packed away. But she had been bitten by the running bug. Although she was not the fastest, she was resolute in her determination and became one of the finest runners in her high school. She went on to run at Calvin College, and in her senior year became All-American. Her name is Heidi Lanning, and she's been an inspiration to many.

Tackle football was out of the question in the school setting, so I invented a game called "Tap Hard and Fall Down," which was a way to circumvent the restriction. The kids swore that if anyone asked, they would never imply that tackling was involved. This was even more fun in the snow and became a favorite winter activity. To this day I still run into kids from the past, now with gray hair, who resurrect stories from those games.

Also in the winter we ran a Saturday basketball clinic. The gym was open to all who wanted to come, and it grew rapidly into controlled chaos. A number of my former students who now played basketball at Unity Christian High School helped me, passing on what they had learned. Some boys who attended the clinic became outstanding players in their own right. I charged the kids a quarter per session and split the loot with my assistants. My take was a sock full of quarters, but it put more bread on the table.

The Jenison area was underserved in the area of recreation, and when I approached the Community Education program representatives with the idea of a soccer program they were encouraging, especially the Community Education director, Dave Bly. I negotiated with Jenison Christian to rent its field for the summer in exchange for having it leveled professionally and adding weed and feed to the combination of gravel and dirt. An advertisement was placed in the local newspaper, and in 1972 Georgetown Soccer was born.

Children between the ages of eight and sixteen were split into four groups of ten on a ten-game schedule. The next year 260 children signed up so I worked with the township to build more soccer fields. My cousin Dave Rodenhouse took me up in his 1946 Aeronca Champ airplane; I hung out over the side taking pictures of potential residential areas that had enough acreage for soccer fields. Then we made arrangements and built the fields.

The kids kept coming. When enrollment approached close to 750 kids I turned it over to AYSO, a national organization similar to Little League. We allowed girls to play with boys, as there were no leagues for girls. I now had time to pursue soccer officiating for high schools and college with great fervor.

I had an internal drive to find things for kids to do. Because these opportunities weren't available when I was a kid, I felt sorry for them. We had made our own fun, but these kids didn't know how to do that. I derived great pleasure in seeing someone do well, and learned how to love kids before I had kids of my own. I was able to turn over to them the love that Grandma DeVries had given me. I'd tell Kay that I couldn't believe I was getting paid to love kids. Soon Kay would also enter the teaching profession.

As a high school student Kay showed the initiative to start her own housecleaning business called Dutch Girl Cleaning Service. Even then she utilized her sense of design by setting up window displays for department stores. At Calvin, since there were no programs suited to her gifts in design, she majored in education, a marketable alternative.

Kay was hired by the Hudsonville school district, and we were so excited when we finally saved up enough money to buy a blue 1973 Mustang. That summer we traveled across the old Route 66 all the way to California. The trip had initially been my idea, but eventually I got cold feet. The prospect of earning some extra money during the summer was more appealing than spending our meager savings, but Kay made the trip happen. I went along grudgingly at first, but we ended up having so much fun. Traveling always expanded our world.

Before we left I bought a tent at MC Sporting Goods (called Michigan Clothiers at that time). When we got to Missouri it was pouring, so we stopped at a KOA. I wanted to sleep in the car, but Kay insisted that I put up the tent. I dug around for the box and pitched that tent in the driving rain. Later in the trip, spending a couple of days in a hippie commune in the foothills of California was a learning experience.

9th grade basketball team, Jenison Christian School, 1973.

John Wooden, Hall of Fame basketball player at Purdue and UCLA coach, was a guest speaker at a coaching clinic at this time. His words resonated with me, and I hoped to speak with him after the presentation. He didn't have time that evening, but he did invite me to join him on an early morning walk. At 6:30 a.m. we walked a brisk two miles while he explained the 1-3-1 zone trap that he so effectively utilized when UCLA won the national championship. I used that scheme in my coaching for the rest of my years at Jenison Christian.

Dr. Bootsma encouraged me to keep my appearance in check, and things went well as long as I was reasonably groomed. He found a job for me plowing snow during the winter and allowed me to drive the snowplow

Marriage and Responsibilities

home. During extended periods of snow, sleep was a scarce commodity and I would often nod off in teacher meetings after a long night of plowing. When I fell asleep while coaching a basketball game, the game was stopped because people thought I'd had a heart attack.

After a ten-period day of teaching elementary PE, the switch to coaching 9th grade boys basketball was a new challenge. We practiced much harder than they had in previous years, but they started to break their habit of losing. The harder we practiced, the harder we played; the harder we played, the more we won. At the end of the year the boys passed a hat and collected $80, which they gave to me at the end-of-season party. The school paid me $100 for the sixteen-game season, so when practice and game time were added up, my earnings were about a dime an hour. The boys' gift meant a lot to Kay and me.

State Champions, Girls Fast Pitch Softball, 1973.

Ken Bootsma pushed me to go to graduate school, which was extremely unappealing because I didn't like school when someone else was teaching. At his urging, I applied to Michigan State University's graduate school, but was devastated when they rejected my application. I couldn't tell him that I had been denied admittance; I found out that I could take classes without being admitted and later reapplied.

A friend and I attended classes all summer in East Lansing. We went to class from 8:30 to 11:30, grabbed a hot dog, hung out by the pool until 1:00, attended class until 4:00, played golf at the Forest Akers Golf Course on campus, went back to class from 7:00 until 10:00, headed across the street to a taco place and went to bed. I couldn't believe this life and wondered often if this would have been possible at Calvin had I applied myself. After earning a 4.0 in several classes I discovered the joy of learning and applied my newfound knowledge to my teaching at JCS.

While taking classes at Michigan State University, two gentlemen took an interest in me and entrusted me to carry out a new methodology of teaching Physical Education. I became great friends with my professor, Dr. Vern Seefeldt, an expert in the correlation of fine motor skills and gross motor skills. He and Dr. John Haubenstricker had conducted research and compiled data on the acquisition and development of motor skills: every activity in which a child engaged was part of a building block; every child was athletically gifted, and their skills needed to reach a certain level of maturity in order for mastery to develop. With this philosophy, they saw the widespread advantages of implementing the Presidential Youth Fitness Commission Program, but did not have access to schools that would carry out their pilot program.

Ken Bootsma allowed me to implement their methodology at Jenison Christian, and a new generation of physical fitness was spawned. At one time Jenison Christian was one of the top schools in the nation in terms of percentages of winners of Presidential Fitness awards. Soon the program was adopted at other non-public schools.

As I became close to earning my masters degree, Dr. Bootsma encouraged me to share my methodologies by making local and statewide presentations, and through a partnership with Christian Schools International I led seminars across the United States and Canada.

Marriage and Responsibilities

During one trip to Canada I was to make a PowerPoint presentation, and I assumed that the Canadian hotel's power grid was the same as ours, but it turned out to be incompatible. So as the technicians worked feverishly to create compatibility, I stood by, hat in hand, with not much to say. From this I learned to always have a backup plan.

Dr. Marv Zuidema, head of Calvin's PE department, asked me to write curriculum. For the next three summers, along with a few other PE teachers, we sat in Calvin's library and wrote K-2, 3-5 and 6-8 curricula, which was later utilized by private Christian schools across the nation. Many colleges sent their student teachers to JCS to observe how we were carrying out the curriculum.

It was also at MSU that I took courses from Dr. George Szypula, the former Hungarian Olympic gymnastic coach from whom I learned spotting techniques, which enabled me to begin a highly successful after-school gymnastics program at JCS that involved hundreds of young girls and a few boys and opened the door to another community recreation program.

Kids were charged fifty cents per session, and soon we raised money for mats, rings and ropes. I donated a trampoline. Since my knowledge of the sport was nonexistent I read books about it and learned along with the kids. Before long, the school became very excited about physical education.

In 1976 I was named Outstanding Young Educator of the Year by the Chamber of Commerce and had the honor of being recognized on a float during the Memorial Day Parade. I instituted the Jenison 10k that took place prior to the parade, which was a big draw.

Rod Smithson and I co-founded the West Michigan Soccer Officials Association and took over the responsibility of assigning officials to games, which ensured a quality experience for the players. At the same time I was becoming more involved with Community Education, so when a position opened for Recreation Director of Georgetown Township, I applied and was hired.

This new job started small but grew like crazy, and before I knew it I was working 55-hour weeks in the summer with the recreation department as well as nights during the school year with the adult program. Kay was at her wits end answering phone calls at all times of the day from players and coaches asking about game locations, from referees calling to cancel, and from part-time high school kids wondering where to get a bag of lime to line the diamonds or reporting that a vandal had driven a car over a softball diamond and damaged sprinkler heads.

As I was driving around town, I saw some young boys on their bikes, jumping curbs and making a nuisance of themselves at the local 7-11. I asked the local bike dealer, Dale Phelps, if he had any ideas about getting them off the streets.

Dale had heard of something called BMX (bicycle motocross) and showed me a magazine that featured the sport. That summer when Kay and I traveled to California to visit relatives and friends we took a side trip to check out BMX and realized it was hot.

Upon returning to Jenison we made a presentation to the township board about the BMX venture. The township attorney was concerned about liability and turned down the proposal. Dale and I took out loans on our homes, borrowed money, rented land, hired Hap Hoekwater and his bulldozer, and Jenison BMX emerged. We brought in a professional rider, Perry Kramer, from Los Angeles, and watched the program explode. Soon we had hundreds of riders each weekend, some coming from Chicago and Detroit to race on the beautiful course. After two glorious years, we sold the operation, and I realized that I'd been bitten by the "for profit" bug.

Dale and I then started the Jenison triathlon, which incorporated swimming, running and biking. The community showed excitement and there was excellent participation from the start.

The thrill of speed combined with a solid bike was something that I had realized at a young age, but my interests had quickly ventured into four-

Marriage and Responsibilities

wheeled vehicles. Since the age of eleven I'd dreamed of owning a Corvette and had put away a few dollars a week in a special fund. Yet after twenty years, when I had finally saved enough to buy the car, I couldn't part with the money. Kay persuaded me to follow through, saying that if I did not buy the car, she would spend the money on something else.

The purchasing arena was just one area in our marriage in which we realized that we both needed to compromise. I needed to be more quick to release, and Kay learned the patience to save. When we finally bought that Corvette and took it home, it became ours.

That summer we flew out to Grants Pass, Oregon, where Kay's family had recently relocated. Spending about six weeks on the farm expanded my world yet again. Days were long and hard, beginning at 6:00 a.m. and ending at 9:00 p.m. After digging ditches, milking cows and working the fields, I found such pleasure in simple things like reading a newspaper that told simple stories about the color of someone's hat at the women's sewing bee.

Big changes were ahead for us. Kay and I had been having serious discussions about starting a family, and as it turned out this trip to Oregon would be our last as a childless couple.

Kids of Our Own and Career Changes

"Feelings of worth can flourish only in an atmosphere where individual differences are appreciated, mistakes are tolerated, communication is open, and rules are flexible - the kind of atmosphere that is found in a nurturing family." - Virginia Satir

Having children was not a decision to be made lightly. My backside had often been the recipient of my dad's short temper, and I never wanted to hit a child. Experience became my role model. I learned by doing, not by observing. My teaching job blessed me with patience, understanding and kindness; it was important that my temper was under control before I had kids of my own.

Another consideration was our finances. Fortunately, a government program reduced Kay's student loans by 10% for every year she taught after the five-year mark.

Kay became pregnant in her fifth year of teaching 4th grade in Forest Grove Elementary School. Her due date was in mid-April. I played in a ball game on a March evening while Kay worked on lesson plans at home. After I went to bed, Kay woke me up to say that she was in labor, and we headed for the hospital.

Months ago we had taken Lamaze classes, which were not very common in those days. Not many dads-to-be were in attendance, but I'm glad that I had the opportunity to extend my coaching experience to the delivery room. Jaime Lynn was born on March 22, 1977.

Since Kay and I were both educators, we'd both taught a lot of little girls, but the inspiration for our daughter's name came from an unlikely source. *The Six Million Dollar Man*, a popular television series at the time, featured Lee Majors as the bionic man. The lead character's name in a spinoff show, *The Bionic Woman*, was Jaime, played by Lindsay Wagner.

Our daughter's birth was the most exciting moment of my life. When I shared the news with Jim Hovinga in his office we both jumped up and down for joy.

The last time I saw Grandma DeVries upright was when we visited her with Jaime.

Four generations: Andy DeVries Jr, Grandma DeVries and Jaime, Andy DeVries Sr.

Kids of Our Own and Career Changes

Jaime became the center of our lives. Kay took five weeks off and then finished the school year. My students at Jenison Christian were thrilled for us and loved to hear Jaime stories; soon my daughter became my frequent companion at school, and she and Kay cheered me on at ball games. Many of our friends also had kids so we had great times raising our children together. To be a part of a community of families meant that there was constant support and always something to do. From 1977 to 1997 we spent a week at Big Star Lake in a cottage with friends.

Families DeVries, Frens, Hovinga, VanderVeen, Hoezee, and VanDyken.

Older women who were eager to help provided exceptional childcare. Men weren't quite as involved in childrearing as they are today, and

I admit that I followed that lead. In addition to her care for the kids, Kay was indispensible in helping me with both of my jobs.

The lot at our home on Pete Street allowed me to put in a sandbox and play structure for Jaime along with a huge garden. I wanted to add onto this house, but Kay convinced me that we could just as easily move to Greenridge, which we did. At our new home in this wonderful neighborhood we built another sandbox and had a garden with fruit trees. No sooner had we moved in when Kay became pregnant again.

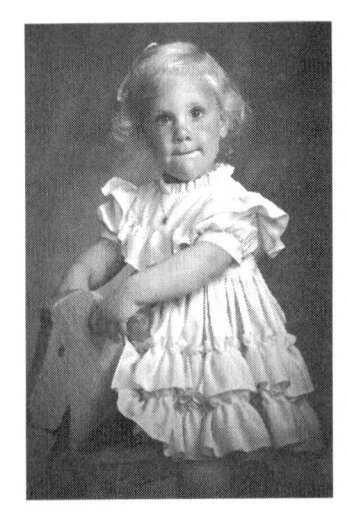

We were convinced that all indicators pointed to a boy this time, but our daughter proved us wrong on May 24, 1980. Naming her was easy, as some of my best gymnasts were named Julie, as were some of Kay's dear students. While Jaime had been an easy baby who hardly made a fuss, poor little Julie had colic and cried a lot. I had an entire wall covered with sound system components including a professional reel-to-reel tape deck. An Elton John song titled "Princess" got Julie and me through that time. We danced to it night after night, I wearing a headset, singing to my crying daughter who was wrapped tightly in my arms.

As I had promised Kay a "real" honeymoon, we made plans for a trip to California for our tenth anniversary in the summer of 1981. Our friends, the Hovingas and the Frenses, asked if they could tag along, so our honeymoon turned out to be a trip for six people. To play on the Pebble Beach Golf Course was on our bucket list. The greens fee was staggering, but we had scrimped and saved, and since it was not a country club I wore my blue jeans. Although we had first-hole jitters, the beauty and grandeur of the course took over, and we had an unforgettable time.

At this time one of my former student teachers provided an

120

opportunity that changed my life. Ron VanderPol had taught in Virginia for a while and later returned to his home state of California to work for his dad, who had a tractor supply company in the San Joaquin Valley. AT&T had a monopoly on long distance services, but a telephone company representative came to their business to sell them what amounted to a long distance package. Ron was convinced that this concept would change the focus of the communication landscape.

ADV and Ron VanderPol.

Ron and a friend of his, Paul Calhoun, put together a business plan and asked if I would join their business. I was becoming a little antsy about the financial cap that could be achieved as a teacher, especially since we were expecting our third child, and tuition for the girls seemed staggering. I expressed hesitancy, but Ron was convincing. Kay and I discussed it, and after a lot of prayer and deliberation with my pastor, I was in.

I asked the JCS school board for a six-month sabbatical, but they said no. I had an exceptional student teacher from Canada, and I wrote lesson plans for the rest of the year and talked to her about taking over so the PE program would not suffer. I went back to the board with another appeal, and was again shot down.

I don't do well when people tell me no, so I quit my job in December of 1983. Kay, even though she was pregnant at the time, was incredible in encouraging me to follow my heart; others, especially fellow teachers, pointed out my stupidity. Leaving teaching was bittersweet, like saying goodbye to an old friend.

Two other friends, Larry VanderVeen and Randy Veltkamp, joined Ron and me to form Teledial America. As former PE teachers, we did not have a business background; we got off to a rocky start and the business went south from there. We were short on equipment, operating capital and everything but good intentions.

I expected that Kay and I would have another girl, so when our son was born on February 27, 1984, I almost fainted. Kay agreed to name him Andrew John III, but wanted to call him Drew instead of Andy. I acquiesced, thinking she'd change her mind eventually. Instead of calling him Drew I stubbornly called him Big Boy for a couple of years. Drew was active. Instead of sleeping he'd roam the halls. He climbed roofs and trees and jumped from high places without a second thought. Kay was at the end of her rope, but since I was working so much I didn't understand what her days were like.

My cycling was a concern for Kay now that we had little ones depending on us, so we agreed to put away the Triumph until they were grown. I was allowed a consolation in the form of a red Yamaha 400, but it just wasn't the same.

Julie catches a ride with her dad on the Yamaha.

I think Kay felt sorry for me when I landed in the hospital with my first kidney stone. The doctors discovered that I had medullary sponge kidney (also known as Cacchi–Ricci disease), a congenital disorder that increases the risk for kidney stones. (This was to be the first stone of many.) The nurse compared my pain level to that of childbirth, so when Kay visited me with the kids they gave me a gift: a pewter statue of a guy on a Harley.

I asked, "Are you saying what I think you're saying?"

My dear wife nixed our prior agreement. My nephew, Nathan, who lived in Florida inherited the Yamaha and I was thrilled to be back on a real bike. However, being a father necessitated that I reevaluate my priorities.

One day I came home to find Kay and little Jaime in the garage with looks of horror and fright on their faces. Jaime had knocked over a stepladder onto my precious Corvette, which sustained countless chips. I went nuts, and because I feared my own reaction I ran around the block again and again until my anger dissipated. When I finally walked into the house I called the *Grand Rapids Press* immediately to place an ad to sell the car. It had become my graven image, almost more important than my family, so it had to go.

While this was going on, I was still preoccupied with a demanding job. The business started at breakneck speed. Right out of the gate we hired people, all of whom needed training. Being more of a big picture person, my skills did not lie in training people for tasks that entailed the exacting mechanical details inherent to the telecommunications industry. I realized quickly what I did not know and took classes to fill the gaps. The American Management Association provided guidance in dealing with people and making key decisions; they taught me how to be assertive rather than aggressive. Pine Rest training courses helped me understand my employees and customers.

I'd stay up late at night, struggling with this new venture, knowing that I was only one day ahead of the people that I had to instruct. We soon oversold our capacity, and the quality of our product wasn't great. My friends were now saying, "I told you so." It was almost as if they delighted in the fact that we were failing. (In retrospect, I believe that if the JCS board had approved my requested sabbatical, I would have quit Teledial after six months.)

I probably learned more in my new career than I had from my other work experiences combined. Driving a truck was a piece of cake. Teaching had been easy. Running the Recreation Department and hiring hundreds of kids each summer was seamless. Planning events for thousands of residents was simple. But every one of these experiences prepared me for new business challenges and for the responsibility of making money rather than spending money that came from another source. When people's livelihoods are dependent upon how they are learning from you, it's a lot of pressure.

With these new responsibilities, every action and decision required deliberation. I learned that you've got to measure your words before you speak. People will hold you accountable for what you say. I learned that life can be hard. I learned humility. I learned how to truly persevere, how to act with passion, and how to respond with praise.

Through all of this I discovered that I was still not prepared. I had to learn on the fly and lead by example, and my character was really put to the test. At times when I became angry I had to sit on it and practice temper control more than ever before.

We soon needed a larger workspace and moved after hours since we didn't contract anything out. We learned how to make a dollar stretch and how to leverage. Looking back, it's amazing how much we learned about the fact that life and business go hand in hand. I learned that in order to be accomplished at selling something you must match people's needs with the product. If you don't have a match, then don't try to push it.

The first couple of years were critical and that's when we made most of our mistakes. Some customers were slow-pay or no-pay. Banks were reluctant to loan money. We did everything from billing to janitorial work; no job was too small. Our employees sensed that we were all in this together, and although things were tough they had an appreciation for what we were doing, so they did not quit.

To complicate matters further, we were selling a new idea to customers. In 1982 the Federal Trade Commission had given AT&T a choice to either break up their monopoly or be broken up, and AT&T decided to do so voluntarily. That left every person and business with a choice that they'd never before had to make.

AT&T's corner on the market seemed solid and steadfast. Their motto was "If it isn't broke don't fix it." Teledial was trying to convince people to do the opposite, swimming against the tide. If we had a slogan it would have been "If it ain't broke, break it."

AT&T continued to use copper wire, which was very expensive, to transmit calls. MCI touted their revolutionary microwave transmission. Sprint had a price advantage. Some companies used satellite transmission. Teledial had a price advantage and the further distinction of being a reseller of the types of services that were offered by other companies. Customers needed clarification, so in an attempt to level the playing field the Chamber of

Commerce presented a full-page article in the *Grand Rapids Press*, the gist of which was that every individual needed to choose a long distance carrier or a decision would be made for them.

The Chamber also offered a seminar in which each company could try to convince the attendees to sign on with their company. Of the four of us who started Teledial, I was the most comfortable with public speaking, so I was chosen to be the spokesman. Still, I was the least qualified because during the time that my partners had attended a telecommunications training session I was training a replacement teacher.

I was completely confused at the seminar. I threw out some terminology and jargon when it was my turn to present, but I really didn't get what we were doing.

A man approached me afterwards and said something to the effect that it seemed that I really did not know what I was talking about.

I asked, "Was it that obvious?"

"It was to me," he answered.

I asked his advice about what to say in front of a group when I was not sure of the answer, and he said that the wisest course was probably to not say anything. I thought about my teaching career. I was the authority then, but in this new forum I was just guessing. From this experience, one of the best lessons I learned was, when in doubt, just keep your mouth shut and let people assume that you know rather than open your mouth and reveal your ignorance.

That brief encounter led me to ask this man, Blake Forslund, to teach me some lessons about business. We met at 1:30 p.m. every Thursday. I later found out that he would come to our meetings straight from the Rotary Club gathering. In 1987 Blake sponsored me into Rotary, which would eventually open many doors for me. He also provided invaluable leads for Teledial, making contacts for us with companies that wouldn't even listen to us before he came on board.

Blake soon took on the role of Drew's surrogate grandfather. When he chartered a fishing boat on Lake Michigan, four-year-old Drew was the token child amongst a bunch of men. On this excursion I finally understood what Kay had been trying to communicate about Drew's high-energy behavior. Captain Jim agreed to allow Drew to catch the first fish. The downriggers were all set, along with sixteen lines. Bang! Drew saw the silver streak of the first fish and grabbed the rod, and we all helped him pull it in when...Bang! Drew let go of the first rod and ran to the second rod.

When the first mate clubbed the first fish, Drew followed suit. I watched with fascination as he jumped from rod to rod and fish to fish. Drew was like a one-man circus, and I finally understood what Kay was dealing with. I had an entire boatload of guys to help me but she did it by herself daily.

At Teledial we learned that the best price does not always result in the best product, and if something is not accomplished today, it might happen tomorrow. But I felt that it was up to me to make it happen, which was a tremendous amount of responsibility. The hardest decisions were those that affected not just us, but many others. The hours were long and the work was never-ending, but after five years of tenuous existence we began to grow.

We began a revolutionary process, running our own fiber ring to transmit calls, the advantages of which were higher capacity and faster speed. We also instituted a creative and logical billing process. Previously, companies charged for long distance by the minute. Even if a phone call lasted five seconds, the customer was charged for a full minute. Teledial figured out a way to charge customers in six-second increments. Companies could also now identify callers through our equipment, which allowed them to bill calls to specific accounts. Our business model resonated with more people each year.

Common Threads: Passion, Perseverance and Praise

One of my responsibilities was to set up new offices and hire personnel as we grew within and outside of Michigan. The necessary travel made the days even longer. To save money I'd stay with employees in their homes. On the road I listened to cassettes that offered advice on how to be a great motivator, learner, listener, salesperson, and manager.

Our budget did not allow for entertaining or advertising. The advertising that we did receive came from trading our services. One of the smartest things we ever did was to become the official long distance carrier for the World Champion Detroit Pistons. In exchange, we received premium seats at the Palace of Auburn Hills and high-visibility promotion. The same deal was made with the Indianapolis Pacers and the Cleveland Cavaliers.

Eventually Teledial America became a household name in the communications industry in Grand Rapids. We were included on the cover of Inc. Magazine as one of the top 100 fastest growing privately held companies in America, a distinction that was achieved for three consecutive years. Michigan Governor John Engler attended the groundbreaking ceremony of our new building at Oak Industrial Drive.

At this point the tagline from my previously skeptical friends changed to "You got lucky." I don't think people understood our level of passion and determination to succeed, or how hard we worked to make it happen. It was also God's grace that had brought us to that point.

Teledial owners rewarded us with gold Gucci watches, when all I'd ever worn before was Timex. We started to feel pretty special. I began to have my suits and shirts custom made and bought one-of-a-kind ties. My corner office in our downtown location overlooked most of Grand Rapids. One day God sent me a powerful message as I rode in the elevator on the way to our 6th floor location.

The Department of Health and Social Services was on a different floor of our building. As I ascended the elevator to our offices, a young minority mother came into the elevator with me, followed by three or four kids, all of whom had runny noses. I flinched when they huddled around me. One of the kids turned and accidentally wiped his nose on my custom-made suit. My immediate response was anger, and I walked the streets to cool off. But then I realized that I was no better than that little boy with the runny nose, and the phrase "There but for the grace of God go I" hit me like a brick. It was a cheap lesson, but an effective one. Nobody knew what had happened except for me, but I was the one who needed the lesson, and I became extremely grateful for what I learned.

In 1989 the Hoops, a Continental Basketball Association franchise, moved to Grand Rapids and caught the town by storm. The dynamic owner, Tom Rubens, had some wonderful ideas about promotions. Some friends and I went in together to become partial owners, which allowed our kids to be involved. Drew and I attended the owners meeting when the mascot, a lime green seven-foot-tall creature, was unveiled. Drew, who was four years old at the time, yelled out "Hoopie!" and the name stuck.

The Hoops played to sellout crowds in the 3500-seat Welsh Auditorium. We had front row seats at every game and followed the team on road trips.

Jaime was awarded an opportunity to be a ball girl. The glamour was that you could rebound for players before the games and at halftimes, but what people didn't see were the arduous hours before and after the games when the ball kids stuffed programs and cleaned locker rooms. They did yeoman work in exchange for the uniform.

The San Diego Chicken visits the Hoops. Drew is the first "chick".

Jaime learned invaluable lessons about punctuality from Tom Rubens' hard and fast rules. If you're a minute late don't bother coming, and if you don't bother coming, you're finished with the job. An additional perk was that she babysat for the players' families and soon Julie took over. It turned out to be a great bookmark in the lives of our kids.

The choice to move the Hoops to the Van Andel Arena in 1996 would be the beginning of the end. The crowd appeared sparse in this 11,000-seat venue, and the excitement of the crowd waned. Before long the franchise started to die. Isaiah Thomas of the Detroit Pistons bought the Hoops and the entire league, but the whole thing would fall apart in 2003.

Kids of Our Own and Career Changes

Blake Forslund, Kay, Joan Forslund, ADV, Earvin "Magic" Johnson, 1994.

Because Teledial had donated generously to the World Vision charity we were invited to Washington, D.C., and given a tour of the White House in 1990. I met with then-Tennessee Senator Al Gore for breakfast, and Kay and I had a delightful evening with Secretary of State James Baker and his wife as we dined and talked about our families.

Common Threads: Passion, Perseverance and Praise

We enjoyed dinner at the White House, complete with the finest linens and official White House china, and behind-the-scenes access to the Smithsonian Institute.

My job was extremely demanding with very long days, but Kay handled most of the details at home, including the caretaking of the kids. On top of all this, she was still teaching in the Hudsonville school district. In retrospect, I had not done well in embracing my wife's needs. I had always worked more than one job, and I projected those same standards onto her.

The kids received an excellent education at Jenison Christian, where I stayed connected and served on the school board. The kids would continue their education at Hudsonville's Unity Christian High School. Throughout their school years they were all active in sports. Jaime especially could not get enough, from biking to roller skating and then to team sports like Little League baseball and soccer.

In every sport in which she participated, Julie had beautiful form. Her movements were so graceful and elegant. In gymnastics, I didn't have to remind her to point her toes; in running and soccer, she ran like a deer; in swimming, her strokes were beautiful. In spite of her ability, she didn't care too much for competition. She found great pleasure in the participation, but not in winning, preferring to stay under the radar.

Drew excelled at soccer, and his form was beautiful to watch. In middle school he became involved in acting. Blake Forslund continued to feed Drew's enthusiasm in the outdoors by taking him hunting and fishing, teaching him to catch and release, and only to kill what he would eat. In high school Drew would discover tennis, eventually winning the Michigan district championship with his doubles partner as well as the Michigan regionals with his soccer team.

The sports arena provided physical benefits for the kids, but also focus and confidence, and I was thrilled to share that connection with them. My dad had never seen me play ball, so I tried not to miss any of my kids' events. They've said that if one person was in the stands or on the sidelines, they knew it would be me. Kay did not enjoy sports as I did, so she went to every other activity; between the two of us, the kids knew they could depend on us.

Grandma and Grandpa DeVries celebrate Julie's 9th birthday.

When Kay and I had children something positive happened regarding the fractured relationship between my dad and me. Although our conversations would always be stilted - we could only talk about the weather and the Detroit Tigers - he became a loving and involved grandfather. I think that as he grew older, as is the case with probably a lot of people, his heart softened.

Common Threads: Passion, Perseverance and Praise

Grandma DeVries' annual pumpkin-carving tradition, 1989.

As my dad had always made sure that our family rented a cottage somewhere for a week, I made sure that my family experienced vacations. Spring break destinations included Disney World and various southern beaches. Florida still held an allure; we'd load up the van and plow straight through the night. We enjoyed ski trips to Colorado, a Caribbean cruise, and a trip to Cancun, Mexico.

Leland, Michigan, 1992.

Kids of Our Own and Career Changes

Accolades and promotions started coming our way at Teledial. In 1994 we were awarded a trip to Scotland and Ireland, the highlights of which were playing at some of the oldest and finest golf courses in the world: Royal Troon, Royal County Down, Lahinch, and St. Andrews. I learned that hard work pays off, and a job well done is recognized and rewarded. You don't do a good job for the reward; the reward is doing the job well.

The History of Golf

Golf has been played on the Links at St Andrews since around 1400 AD and the Old Course is renowned throughout the world as the Home of Golf. The game grew in popularity and by the 19th century it was part of the way of life for many local people, whether as players, caddies, ball makers or club makers. Golf still plays a major part in the culture and economy of St Andrews today.

As the 600-year history of the Links has unfolded, one simple track hacked through the bushes and heather has developed into six public golf courses, attracting hundreds of thousands of golfing pilgrims from around the globe. St Andrews Links is the largest golfing complex in Europe and all five 18-hole courses can be booked in advance.

Bunkers on the Old Course are infamous: ADV and Frank Tidmarsh.

Golf was clearly becoming popular in the middle ages, and the game was banned in 1457 by King James II of Scotland who felt it was distracting young men from archery practice. This ban was repeated by succeeding monarchs until James IV threw in the towel and in 1502 became a golfer himself.[10]

The Royal and Ancient Golf (R&A) Club at St. Andrews is considered the governing authority of the sport. The Professional Golfers' Association (PGA) and the United States Golf Association (USGA) interpret the rules that have been established by the R&A.

Frank Tidmarsh and ADV, the Old Course, 1994.

My caddy, Frank Tidmarsh, was unassuming, meticulous and dignified, a true Scottish gentleman. I was almost more focused on him than the game because his stories of World War II service and Scottish history were so fascinating. He asked me to join him for a "spot of tea" afterwards, graciously offering that my friends could come along, but they gave me grief that I chose this invitation instead of hitting the pubs with them.

I gave Mr. Tidmarsh a chance to change and was shocked when he emerged from the R&A Headquarters in a suit and a tweed hat. It turned out that he was the R&A Secretary; he only caddied one day a month for fun. Frank took me up to the seat from which Queen Elizabeth watched the final round of the British Open. From there he showed me the queen's private ninepin bowling lane and the world's first golf ball, tees, and clubs. He even gifted me with a periwinkle vest that featured the official R&A crest. When I met my friends, needless to say, they regretted their decision to turn down Frank's invitation to tea.

For the last two days of the trip Kay and I traveled to Friesland, the Netherlands, to search for my grandparents' homes and connect with cousins whom we'd never met. We found the Dantuma Slagery (butcher shop), owned by Grandma DeVries' sister's family. As the Netherlands was playing Brazil in the World Cup that week, the shop was elaborately festooned and buzzing with activity. As I waited to speak to a relative I noticed a picture on a corkboard of my grandma holding me as an infant.

My relatives told the story of how my father and Uncle Bud, on leave from World War II service, had borrowed an Army vehicle and driven all the way to Friesland to connect with them. While there, some rebels in the clan siphoned gas from their automobile. Times were tough during the war and everything was rationed, so stealing even from relatives was apparently justified by some. In Amsterdam we found a storefront that bore Kay's surname, Grond.

When we returned to the United States a friend of mine, J.C. Huizenga, shared with me his vision to begin a charter school. As things were progressing, I told him that if he invested in this venture I would assist him on the professional side. People with a variety of philosophies were also instrumental: John Booy, a teacher in the Grand Rapids Public Schools and later a co-founder of Potter's House School; Meg Cusack, who brought years of homeschooling expertise; Sid Jansma of Wolverine Gas and Oil, and Kris Mauren, Executive Director of the Acton Institute. The first board was heavily tilted toward the common greater good. Although some of us could afford private education for our own children, we wanted something better for those who did not have or choose that option.

The drive behind forming this organization was our concern for the state of public education. My business had trouble finding capable graduates from public schools. Kids from private schools and suburban public schools went on to college, but some kids from the inner city public school system weren't able to communicate effectively with customers, did not have adequate mathematical skills, and did not have the common sense that we expected of those who held high school diplomas.

J.C. is involved with many businesses but he's a man with a heart for the underdog, and he had in me a partner with the same philosophy. The value that my ancestors had placed on education was also an impetus for me to stand behind this idea. The founders of this group believed that everyone in America has a right to a solid education, and we felt that since some public schools were not delivering, it was necessary to provide that possibility. We needed to level the playing field of educational opportunities.

The original name of the organization was the Education Development Corporation. A professional public relations company came in for a weekend to come up with a more suitable name. They decided on three words: National, to communicate that this would grow beyond Michigan;

Kids of Our Own and Career Changes

Heritage, to show that the intent was to reach back with values and morals; and Academy, to evoke a more serious academic image. NHA would be the acronym for the organization.

NHA was successful right out of the gate. After our charter was granted, we rented space that used to be a doctor's office. So many families applied that we had to have a lottery drawing.

The lobby of the Bridgewater Place downtown was filled with families, and each child was assigned a number. Parents crossed their fingers, arms and legs when the lottery machine randomly popped up numbers, hoping that their kids' numbers would be chosen. If one child in a family was selected, the siblings also were assured of a spot. The first K-8 school was named Excel Charter Academy.

J.C. Huizenga, ADV, Pete Rupert, first NHA golf outing, 1995.

NHA has continued to fulfill needs in many communities, adding new schools all over the United States every year, and I strongly believe that our goal of providing an exceptional education to all students is being accomplished.

Grand River Preparatory High School has been in existence since 2008, offering a topnotch secondary education that ensures a smooth transition to college. It has been a privilege to serve as the President of the boards of Excel Charter Academy and Grand River Prep for many years.

National Heritage Academies: A Foundation Built on a Parent's Perspective

It was the birth of his son that inspired National Heritage Academies' founder, J.C. Huizenga, to begin thinking about education from a parent's perspective. A successful entrepreneur, Huizenga had a vision to provide a quality education to all children by applying basic business principles to establish a system of schools that was more accountable and results oriented. National Heritage Academies' first school, Excel Charter Academy, opened its doors to 174 students in September 1995.

NHA has become a national leader serving more than 48,000 students in 76 schools across nine states. Founded on the pillars of rigorous academics, a moral-focused environment, academic excellence, and individual student responsibility, NHA schools are impacting the lives of students in measurable ways. NHA continues to partner with communities to open new schools with a vision to better educate more children. National Heritage was listed in Inc. magazine's "500 Fastest Growing Private Companies," four different times.[11]

*Excel Charter Academy groundbreaking, 1998.
Photo courtesy of Maryanne Bartell.*

Teledial sprung for a trip to Hawaii in 1996. We golfed at the majestic Kapalua Bay Course surrounded by palm trees and hibiscus while dolphins frolicked in the Pacific Ocean nearby.

Hawaii, 1996.

Company owners sought opportunities for growth, but decisions that were made for the sake of expediency ended up hurting many people. We merged with a company in Detroit in 1995, and even at the beginning it did not feel like a good match. The new partners did not seem to conduct business the way we were used to doing it.

Soon after the merger our companies came together for a Christmas party. At previous parties, an officer from our company would always read a passage of Scripture. At this party, someone from the new company read an inane secular passage, and it became immediately apparent that this company did not share our value system. The growth to which we had become accustomed now took a different direction. We made bad marketing and hiring decisions, and work became a challenge instead of a joy. My confidence started to erode, especially when one of the new leaders attempted to drive a wedge between the majority owner and me.

Kay and I had started building a house and were stretched financially. Jaime was ready to graduate from high school and Drew was starting middle school. Life was very hard, partly because I foolishly tried to keep the truth from Kay and my family. I did complain a bit, and Kay could tell that something was not right, but I did not elaborate. I did what had always worked in the past: I put my head down and worked harder. This was a time when perseverance was probably a mistake. In retrospect I should have quit, but I was chasing a jaded dream.

Work became even more difficult. The majority owner wanted to give the new president full rein to show his trust even though he was not aware of how things were being handled. I was removed from the board and lost my position of authority. Being marginalized was horrifying, and I was paralyzed by indecision. New employees were blinded by new leadership's promises of quick riches. The direction was self-serving instead of profit-making and did not mesh with the lives that we were called to live.

When I finally told the majority owner what was going on he became incensed and the new president was fired. Our old president returned, and acquisition negotiations began with a company from Ohio called LCI International.

Financially, the timing was right to sell the company. I was contracted to stay with a no-compete agreement. My job was to ensure that our customers' sales contracts would continue. I was working for a company that I didn't believe in, selling something that I didn't believe in, and it felt like I was living a lie. This was hands down one of the most difficult years of my life, but I took it personally and had difficulty sharing. I regretted many decisions, and since I was unhappy with life I'm sure that I was very hard to live with.

Despite struggles at work, there were many bright spots in my personal life. When Drew was in middle school we had an opportunity to pilot a B-29 bomber, the *Aluminum Overcast*, with the original WWII crew on a flight over Lake Michigan. This was especially meaningful because of Uncle Bob's history flying B-29s during WWII.

The Aluminum Overcast

Spectrum Health hospital began testing a helicopter that would eventually be used to transport individuals from accidents scenes and other hospitals to their own facility. Before the helicopter is considered operational it undergoes a "shakedown" process, which is a period of testing and trial runs.

Blake Forslund, who was on the Spectrum board at the time, invited me to accompany him, his wife Joan, and fellow board member Bill Martindale on the maiden voyage. I had no idea that I would myself be a patient on the AeroMed a few years later.

After I had secured long-term contracts for most major customers at LCI, I made a decision to quit even before the bonuses were paid. This turned out to be one of the happiest days of my life. It may have been financially foolish to leave when I did, but it was important for my emotional sanity.

For my 50th birthday Kay purchased a road trip to Arizona through Harley-Davison's Fly and Ride program. Available to members of the H.O.G. (Harley Owners Group), this allows cyclists to fly to various locations in and out of the United States and rent a bike at a local Harley dealership to tour the area. I met my college roommate Jene Vredevoogd and we enjoyed the splendor of the Grand Canyon and mountains of the west.

In my first business career I had learned that things are not always what they appear to be. People don't necessarily have your best interests in mind. Although God has a plan, you have a responsibility to perform the due diligence that's required to carry out the plan. Don't assume. Do your homework, don't cut corners, and make sure you are well prepared.

After I left LCI a friend of mine who also had a penchant for soccer heard that indoor soccer was growing in popularity. The YMCA on the southwest side of Grand Rapids had fallen to disrepair; the building was like a maze, and annexes had been added on as afterthoughts. My friend put up the cash, and we redesigned the building and brought indoor soccer to West Michigan, calling it the Sports XChange. We added a food court, putt-putt golf, volleyball, and basketball. The novelty of the business ensured that it was a hit right out of the gate.

The business seemed like a natural fit for our family, as the kids were very sports-minded. I continued to officiate as well as play on various teams, including a traveling volleyball team that included guys from several Midwestern states.

The Bullfrogs, 1998.

I was honored to serve as Rotary President while my new career was getting off the ground. Being involved in Rotary since 1987 had allowed me to form connections with Grand Rapids business leaders such as Skip Baxter, Chuck Stoddard, Dick Young, and Scott Brinkmeyer. Blake Forslund's mentorship had been even more invaluable during the arduous Teledial years. I think most Rotarians knew what I was going through. They were incredibly helpful, and this had allowed me to find the silver lining at a very difficult time.

Going through the Rotary ranks also afforded opportunities to travel and meet people from other countries. I gained wider perspective and learned that the world is not Grand Rapids.

ADV, International Rotary President Luis Vincente Giay from Argentina.

One of my duties as President was to meet and greet our speakers, such as former Michigan governor George Romney. Over coffee at the Amway Grand Plaza he asked what motivated me, and I explained that I had done my best to help the underachieving and the underserved such as students in the Grand Rapids Public Schools. He shared that he was beginning a foundation that had that same goal and asked what kinds of problems I was encountering. I said that the more I helped these students, the more they seemed to expect. I was taking them to the YMCA and to lunch but it didn't seem that I was making any headway. Governor Romney said something that will stick with me for the rest of my life.

"Andy, you can throw money at a problem for the rest of your life, and at the end of your life you'll have an empty wallet. But if you give time, you'll change a life."

From that point on, instead of trying to buy a relationship, I earned it. The money that I spent had little effect. When I provided homework assistance at schools and helped students graduate, it made a difference.

Blake Forslund, U of M's Bo Schembechler, ADV.

Another lesson that I soon learned was that you should never try to be something that you're not. My partner and I allowed a struggling private school to use the Sports XChange building during the day. We learned that it is difficult to combine for-profit organizations with not-for-profit, especially when the not-for-profit takes what you've given them for granted. It would have been lucrative to bring in various charter schools and homeschoolers for an organized PE experience, and we had people lined up, but the private school was given full access the entire day. It became a tenuous relationship.

To further utilize the space and increase profitability we sponsored lockdowns for high school senior graduating classes, for which we provided concessions and brought in special equipment. This was fun but it did not do enough to carry us.

When we brought in a professional soccer team called the Grand Rapids Explosion our responsibilities included everything from locating playing fields to generating press releases. We found places for the players to live and procured summer jobs for them. I should have learned from my first foray in business not to assume anything. It turned out that the general manager was siphoning money, so this venture came to a close.

Putting this experience in perspective, I needed those three years to regain my confidence. I'd been so verbally beaten up in the last years of my prior career and my confidence had been so shaken; although the indoor soccer experience was not wildly successful overall, it was a lot of fun. I realized that I could bounce back.

At the same time that we decided this business could not be a viable entity, Calvin College was beginning to expand their internship program. I was offered a split job in 1999 to teach Marketing 380 in the business department and to jumpstart the effort to promote. When I joined the faculty only a few students were placed in internships per semester, and not many professors at that time had business connections. The business department really wasn't pushing for expansion of the internship program, but the wider community understood the necessity. My job was to delineate expectations for the interns and the businesses. It was an inexpensive way for businesses to get a head start on future employees, to build loyalty, and to avoid the tedious process of hiring through the Human Resource department.

Teaching again was so much fun and made my spirits soar. I remembered riding my motorcycle to campus on my first day of college all those years ago with my head in the clouds, and I was so grateful for what Calvin had done for me. I hoped to do the same thing for the many others who were struggling. It turned out to be a fabulous place to work; I had opportunities to teach, connect with businesses, and build my own career. Being a part of Calvin allowed me to apply my regained confidence in a positive way.

I discovered a great love for Calvin in the business community, and people started to give back. They noticed that Calvin was not merely a liberal arts college, it was also an institution that was serious about business. I started a group called the Calvin Business Alliance comprised of thirty business leaders in the area who had Calvin College connections. We met semiannually and discussed how we could foster growth for our beloved institution.

Our team (sponsored by Yesterdogs) won the USA Open in 2000.

My life was still so caught up in sports; some weeks I played ball almost every night. When we were dating, Kay had gone to all the games, and I foolishly assumed that it was because she enjoyed them. In reality she was going only to see me, and she didn't watch much of the games. I thought that when we married, Kay would continue to attend the games, but she thought that I'd put away my childish actions and be a fulltime husband. We were both surprised. I continued to play ball and Kay stopped going.

As our volleyball team became more competitive we traveled all over the United States. Winning crucial games got the adrenaline pumping, and I thought I was on top of the world. I don't remember Kay ever attending a volleyball game. Someone had to hold down the fort, and she did.

In the summer of 2000 Julie had an internship at Snow Mountain Ranch in Estes Park, Colorado. I was asked to make a presentation to the interns about careers, and afterwards Julie and I took some time to explore the majestic Rocky Mountains on my motorcycle.

My friends and I had another opportunity in September of 2001 to play golf on more of Europe's most iconic courses, including Ballybunion, Turnberry, Carnoustie, Loch Lomand, Royal Portrush and Lahinch.

Kids of Our Own and Career Changes

LarryVanderVeen, Randy VanDyken, Rick VandenBerg, ADV, Royal and Ancient Headquarters, 2001.

At the St. Andrews starters shack I asked if Frank Tidmarsh, my caddy from our trip in 1994, was still around. They said he'd quit caddying but gave me his phone number. I connected with him and he rode his bike to the course to caddy one last time at the age of eighty-five. This time I carried the bag.

In the middle of our round at Royal County Down in Newcastle, Ireland, we were informed that the Twin Towers in New York City had been hit by airplanes.

My caddy said to me, "America will never be the same. Your country has now experienced terror, and now we are on an even keel."

We spent a tense week trying to get back to the United States as we witnessed the horror of this heinous event from the perspective of Europe. Armed policemen at Heathrow Airport were a constant reminder of fear.

We also saw human nature in full force as hoteliers engaged in price gouging to capitalize on tourists' desperation. We crammed eight guys in a room for two. The lesson was that no place is impervious to terror.

Our volleyball team played in a crucial tournament in 2001. Winning this tournament allowed us to qualify for the nationals, and I soon traveled to Saginaw to try out for the Seniors Master Olympics. I could never have imagined the turn that my life was about to take.

Brushes With Death Bring Abundant Life

"One way to define wisdom is the ability to see, into the future, the consequences of your choices in the present. That ability can give you a completely different perspective on what the future might look like." – Andy Andrews, The Noticer

Jene Vredevoogd and I took a cycle trip on September 14, 2002, to Saugatuck. On the return trip I was involved in an accident that would become a turning point in many ways.

As we traveled east on 32nd Street in Holland, a motorist ran a red light at Highway 31 and T-boned me, pulverizing my left leg between her bumper and my engine.

My body flew through the air, and after my right shoulder smashed through the car's windshield, I bounced off the hood and ended up on the highway. The car rode over my right leg.

Jene parked his bike to block traffic and called 911 with his cell phone. When the emergency vehicle workers arrived and saw the condition of my leg, they prepared to carry me into the ambulance. Jene, concerned that I had sustained a head injury, insisted that a backboard be used to transport me. In that decision he may have saved my life.

The physicians at the Holland Hospital were unprepared to deal with the magnitude of my injuries so I was taken to Spectrum Hospital on the AeroMed.

My leg looked like a slab of meat. Most of the ligaments around my knee had been severed, so absent of anything to keep my kneecap in place, it ended up by my hip. That evening in the ER my knee was reconstructed; ligaments were pulled down from the groin to reattach the kneecap. A titanium rod was put in to keep it all in place.

Four days after the accident the doctors were astounded that my leg was still "alive" without a vein to provide blood flow. The only source of blood was a capillary to my pinky toe, but soon it was determined that the blood flow was not adequate. My orthopedic surgeon, Cliff Jones, scheduled an amputation, and I marked the leg with a permanent marker. A chance conversation with Drew caused Dr. Jones to reconsider.

Drew told Dr. Jones, "My dad is a fighter. He would work harder than anyone else to get that leg to function again."

"If I have to, I can take the leg off tomorrow," said Dr. Jones, "but I can never put it back on."

Over the next days small improvements occurred, but this time opposition came in the form of my gastroenterologist, who insisted that my liver was not strong enough to sustain the pressure from anesthesia that would be required for additional surgeries. He said the leg had to go, but his advice was not heeded.

Skin was grafted from my healthy leg. My weight shot up to over 280 pounds because I was retaining fluid, and my skin turned black, which was not a good sign. Debridement became the next course of treatment, in which dead and damaged tissue is continually removed in order to increase potential for healing.

During one hospital stay things looked quite grim, and the doctors suggested that our kids come in. I was not aware of their presence, but as they surrounded my bed I had a vivid glimpse of heaven.

In this vision I remember being an observer before I was a participant. I saw a vast panoramic field in which the landscape, the fir trees and the sky were very pale. Color began to come in slowly. The sky was now a pastel blue, and the tree trunks and branches began to fill out. There was movement on the wildflowers of the grassy plain. On the far right I also noticed that a small stick figure had come into the picture. It looked like a scarecrow.

The colors started to deepen and gradually became vibrant. I could even see the details in the tree bark. The foliage was forest green and the sky was bluebird blue. The wildflowers were every imaginable color - yellows and oranges, blues and violets. Every color of the rainbow was expressed in that floral arrangement. A wind caused the flowers to wave like the sea.

When the colors were at their most vivid, the stick figure started to move toward the center and began to take shape. Bones took on muscle and muscle took on flesh. The body moved more smoothly and clothes appeared. His shirt was one like I had worn when I was younger. It had blue and white alternating stripes, three buttons, and a henley collar. The man wore jeans and Docksiders. He started to skip. One thing I had learned from teaching was that the happiest form of movement is skipping. It is rare to see a child who is skipping and not smiling. That figure in my vision had adapted to a movement style of happiness.

At that point I felt a hand gripping my ankle. I shook my head and yelled "No!" and the figure in my vision suddenly vanished, colors went pale, and everything disappeared. I instead felt as if I were enclosed in a white tube, and I heard a loud "whoosh." I opened my eyes and saw my son's face. Drew was at my bedside, and I was jolted back to reality.

The meaning of that vision was so clear to me. I was entering heaven in my broken body. It was as if I had arrived, only to be pushed back to earth. I realized that God had more for me to do.

Constrained as I was, I had nothing but time on my hands. I was completely dependent on Kay, yet her feelings for me were understandably not completely positive. While before I could always carry on, I was now completely helpless. I vowed to change if and when I had the opportunity, but I was at a loss regarding how to improve our relationship.

Drew played on Calvin's soccer team that fall. Kay and I had watched his first three games before the accident, but I could no longer be the supportive dad that I wanted to be. At that time it was thought that I was dying, which made things even more difficult for Drew.

As a further tribute to the Calvin community, the rest of the soccer games were taped and delivered to my hospital room by the coaches so I could watch them. I'll never forget being driven from the hospital to the Calvin soccer field where I watched (wrapped in blankets and in a wheelchair) as Drew played the best game he's ever played in his life in a win against Central Michigan University, a Division 1 team.

Music has always been a huge part of my life, but during my recuperation I experienced a spiritual revival. Listening to the blues or rock music was not soothing, but songs about God and Jesus and what's coming next were a comfort. Gospel music brought me close to God, and I'd sing until I was wet with tears. I'll never forget how it got me through my deepest, darkest moments and will always be grateful.

I was transferred to Metro Hospital for rehab, ostensibly to learn how to live and function in a wheelchair. I can't say enough about the encouragement that was provided by the Spectrum staff, especially Sarah Scholl. (See *Grand Rapids Press* article, page 210.) I was determined to walk, partly because of Sarah's challenge and partly because I'm so competitive.

In October I took my first steps, aided by a walker. In addition to learning how to dress myself, figure out medications, tone the upper body muscles that were starting to waste away, and bend and stretch everything in my lower body, I sat in "group" with four or five other elderly patients. Some of the patients had undergone knee replacement surgery and some were suffering from West Nile virus. In our wheelchairs we kicked at beach balls and did other simple exercises. Motivational awards were given. One was a field trip to Robinette's Orchard. That was the last place I wanted to go.

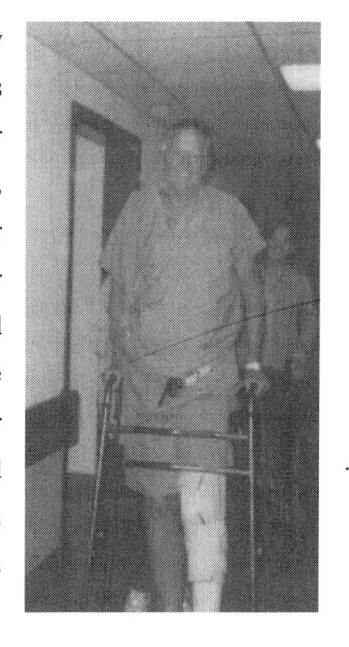

The therapists pushed hard for me to make the trip and I acquiesced. A short bus, the kind that picks up handicapped children, transported us that morning. I was locked in place in my wheelchair. Our daughter Jaime went with me. I didn't have proper clothes, only pajamas and a bed sheet.

It seemed like everyone was watching me. I used to be normal but now I had special needs. We arrived and unloaded. I wheeled my chair off the bus lift and headed for the front door of the building. The door opened with an outward pull. I couldn't reach the handle because my leg was sticking out straight. There was no way I could get into the building.

I think that's why the therapists sent us there. Many places claim to be handicapped accessible, but once you become handicapped you realize that the architects have little idea of what accessible really means. I fought my way inside, sweating profusely. Now what? Everyone else had a wallet. I was in my pajamas. I hadn't spent money in a month since I'd been in the hospital for the past thirty days.

I wanted to get out of the store, so I started wheeling my way down a too-narrow aisle. My hands bumped into things that were stacked on the shelves. My leg knocked over an entire end cap of potato chips as I turned the corner. I was so embarrassed at the mess I was making and just wanted to get out. Everyone else wanted to stay, so majority ruled.

I went outside and found myself careening down a slight grade. I lost control of my chair and started rolling toward certain doom. As I came closer to the end of the sidewalk and the wall at the end, I prayed that someone would help me. I saw my life flash in front of me as I imagined another broken leg after I hit the wall. A rescuer did appear and rushed to catch my runaway chair. Through that trip I learned many lessons about judging others before you walk in their shoes.

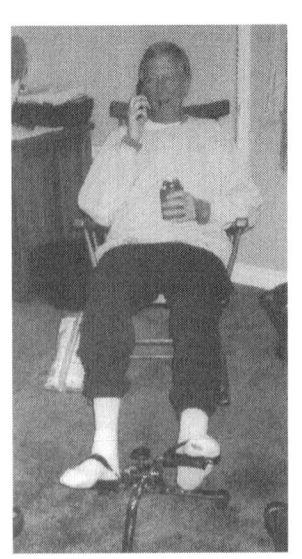

When I was released from Metro it was wonderful to be finally home, but rehab was still intense. Rotary members and friends Blake Forslund, Chuck Stoddard, Dick Young, Ed DeVries, Jim Schreiber, John Grant, and Tom and Grace Shearer proved to be invaluable supporters. My cousins Bob, Ken, Dave and John visited often and encouraged me every step of the way. Our Bible study group met at my home.

Shortly after I moved back home I received an ironic letter informing me that I'd been chosen for the Masters Olympic team representing Michigan and Indiana. The coach, John Wilder, could have taken me off the roster, but instead showed incredible compassion by offering me an opportunity to play if I could merely stand and serve. I asked Kay if she would attend the game and she said yes. To think of Kay watching me play volleyball made me work harder than I ever had before.

Getting out the door for the first time without Kay was brutal, but my friends knew that it was essential to my health and wellbeing. Larry VanderVeen and Bob Evenson picked me up to see the Stanley Cup in the Van Andel Arena, won by the Detroit Red Wings in February 2003. They had arranged with the Griffins top brass for me to hold the trophy while I was sitting in the wheelchair.

My new intensive regimen included water therapy in a local pool three times a week. Before the initial class we entered the pool, awaiting our instructor, Glenda. As we hung to the edge of the deep pool and kicked mightily to keep afloat, I asked the other nine participants if they looked forward to returning to work. The responses were everything from "No" to "Hell, no." They were all collecting workmen's compensation and planned to keep it that way. This mentality was a shock. The instructor brought in Motown music and pushed me to relearn balance with the help of Smokey Robinson and Martha and the Vandellas. I was motivated to prove my liver specialist wrong, more determined than ever that I would walk again.

The Masters Olympics tournament was held in Virginia Beach. The drive took twenty hours because Kay and I had to stop every hour. She helped me out of the car from my reclining position in the back seat so I could move around and stretch.

I didn't expect to play. One of my teammates took a page from the movie *Rudy* and started to chant, "An*dy*, An*dy*" and soon everyone joined. The coach called me in to serve. I threw the ball up, and out of the corner of my eye, while the ball was in the air, I looked in the stands and saw Kay. It was one of those moments in which time stops.

My wife had stood by me through everything, and here she was by my side making this happen. I lost it. At that moment it dawned on me that, through my accident, God was teaching me a lesson about what was important in life. Volleyball had become my idol. Competing at a high level wasn't what God had intended for me. What he did intend for me was to be a good husband and father.

Tears welled in my eyes. They came so fast and I tried to I blink them out, but I could not see the ball. I swung and hit the ball with my thumb. The ball landed a couple of feet into the court. This was the Olympics and there was no do-over, so I was horribly embarrassed. But I was also kind of grateful. A lot of questions were answered in that brief moment. I learned that some things in life were more important than things that were merely good for me.

The coach told me to stay in the game, and I was able to hop on one leg through the rest of it. I became a back row attack player, and we won the game. We continued to be undefeated, and at that point the coach made a wise decision to take me out.

Our team won the semifinals. Before the final game we stood in a circle and put our hands together in the middle. The coach said, "This one's for Andy." We won the game handily and became the Masters Olympics

Champions of 2003.

The weight of that medal around my neck was exciting, but even more thrilling was the realization that this experience was not one that would stand the test of time. That moment was a turning point in our lives. I realized that the accident that had almost taken my life had saved my marriage.

As I continued to heal from the accident, a hereditary liver condition, congenital hepatic fibrosis, became exacerbated because of the trauma that my body had experienced. The onset of symptoms associated with this condition can strike at any time, but as I was concentrating on healing from the accident, my concern about the liver condition was momentarily pushed to the back burner.

In a healthy body, the blood that leaves the stomach and intestines goes through the liver to be cleansed. The liver breaks down the nutrients and excretes bile, which carries away waste material. With hepatic fibrosis, toxins accumulate in the bloodstream because the blood is not properly cleansed by the damaged liver.

One of the symptoms when this occurs is hepatic encephalopathy, in which cognitive ability and memory are compromised.

Drew was a student in one of my classes at Calvin. He told Kay that I didn't seem to be as sharp as usual.

A colleague, Bob Eames, sat in a class session and told me, "Andy, sometimes you're not making any sense. You're not cohesive."

For the rest of the semester he sat in and we had a code.

If I was off my game he would say, "Professor DeVries, I need a break." That was his way to tell me that I was not making sense.

I would follow up with, "Perhaps the students would like a break, too."

Bob would then finish the class and I'd go home. The encephalopathy worsened, and I was aware that my teaching was adversely affected. Calvin assigned another professor, Deb Kiekover, to team teach with me the following semester.

It's a tribute to Calvin that they did not disable me or withhold my pay. Instead they put me on hold and extended incredible support. I joined the Development department as Director of Corporate Giving. Calvin was gracious to give me the freedom to figure out what I needed to do.

I can't say enough about what I learned about Calvin's sense of community during my time in rehab after the accident. What made it even more poignant was that it was so different from what I'd experienced in the business world. Even though the companies were faith-based and had good people, the environment at Calvin College trumped anything I'd previously seen.

I was warned by my doctors to look for symptoms of an esophageal bleed, and it occurred while I was working at Calvin. So many things that happened during that afternoon point to God.

Since my liver was rock hard and damaged, it could no longer accept or cleanse any blood. My body tried to create new pathways, but this could only continue for so long. Eventually the vein bursts, and the excess bleeding is evident in blackened stools.

Although I had been looking for symptoms, I did not recognize them when they came. I was working late on a sunny Friday afternoon, and everyone else had gone home for the day. I went to the bathroom and noticed that my stool was black as tar, but I thought it must have been something I ate. Fifteen minutes later I returned to the bathroom with what appeared to be diarrhea, again black as tar. The same thing happened several minutes later.

A fellow employee, Bob Berkhof, returned to the office and remarked that I did not look very well. I told him I'd been having diarrhea. He asked me what seemed like a very outlandish question.

"What color is it?" he asked.

I told him it was black and he said, "That's blood."

I realized at that moment that this was exactly what I was supposed to be looking for, but it had never dawned on me. I was bleeding to death.

I continued to bleed and my gastroenterologist, Dr. Michael Puff, was able to locate and patch the rupture in my veins. The doctors told me that my only chance of survival would be a liver transplant.

Many additional surgeries were necessary to buy time while I waited, including transjugular intrahepatic portosystemic shunts (TIPS) procedures to create new connections between blood vessels in the liver. Kay and I made countless trips to Ann Arbor for treatments and tests. During each visit, blood was drawn to assess a MELD (Model for End-Stage Liver Disease) score. This score indicated the level of liver damage and determined how soon I would be eligible to receive a transplant. While in Ann Arbor I was required to participate in group meetings with patients who had the same condition. Speakers gave us a realistic understanding about how difficult this road would be, and some of the patients' health declined before my very eyes. This only made me more anxious to receive a transplant quickly.

My first mentor Bill Carlson would visit with me at home with his twin brother, Bob. Bob told stories of Anna Maria Island, where he and his wife had purchased a home. Kay and I looked it up and decided to take a trip, even though I was not doing well.

We looked at a condo on a canal with a boat slip but were not very impressed until Bob took us to the most beautiful beach I'd ever seen. Although Florida had always been a place of tremendous memories for me and for our family, at that point I wasn't sure that I'd survive even if I did receive a transplant. Nevertheless, I purchased the condo with the thought that this beautiful nook would be a place for Kay to visit if I died.

The view from the Anna Maria Island condo.

Kay did an exhaustive search to find out where most liver transplants took place and discovered that Indianapolis was our best bet. In August of 2006 we found an apartment a couple of blocks from the transplant facility in Indy. We settled in and waited for the gift of life.

Calvin College, in its infinite goodness, allowed me to ostensibly continue my work. Indianapolis was not the region to which I was assigned, but I was given a long list of people to contact, and it gave me purpose. One person on the list was Gary Schipper, the minister of the only Christian Reformed Church in Indianapolis.

Gary and I met at an English pub and at first made some idle chitchat. I mentioned to him that it was almost difficult to look forward to a transplant, because I knew that it would happen only if someone else died. It made me think of Christ's sacrifice for us.

Gary said, "It sounds like you have a lot of people that are coming to see you. Why do you think that is? Grand Rapids to Indy is a ten-hour round trip. You must do something to build a relationship with them."

I said that I ask them about what's going on in their lives. I ask them,

"What's up?" If they claim that nothing is going on, I push for more information.

He asked, "How's your relationship with God?"

I realized that I was in awe of God and I believed that he saved me, but I was on the receiving end and not on the giving end. In my prayers I found myself thanking and asking. If I treated a friend in that way, it would be a pretty shallow relationship.

Gary challenged me to be more purposeful in my conversations with God and to give more. I was troubled, but it was an enabling thought - did I dare try?

Our apartment was on a canal. There was a lot of ambient light at night; even with shades closed, the red and blue lights of the police cars and fire engines flashed through. In my bed that night I took a chance. I said, "Okay God, what's up?"

The room suddenly became very dark. The only other time I'd experienced that kind of palpable darkness was in the Mammoth Caves of Kentucky. Then a wind came. It wasn't a breeze through the window, but rather a force that came from the direction of the inner wall. I felt the wind on the hairs of my arm. To take a page from the Bible, I was sore afraid.

On the wall in front of me appeared a grey rectangle the size of a big screen television. It looked white in contrast to the surrounding blackness. A three-inch-wide black line started to move up from the base of the rectangle. A vertical line moved across from the left side, crossing the horizontal line. At the base of the vertical line a tubular figure emerged at a 45-degree angle. At its top, something popped out, like a tulip at the end of a stem. An eye and a nose appeared, finally developing into a face - my face, looking at me.

I had finally been able to be direct with God, and there I was in the shadow of the cross. I quickly woke up Kay, but everything went back to normal, and she didn't see it.

That vision brought me such peace. To my question, "What's up,

God?" he had answered, "I'm here, saving you." It was so incredibly concise and clear. Since then I have had no fear of death.

Spending time in Indy was a defining period in our lives because for the first time, Kay and I had to leave Grand Rapids and rely on each other for help. We attended a church in which the congregants were black and the pastor was white. The support was overwhelming; the congregation prayed fervently for a donor as we waited.

The church space was used by many denominations: the Church of Christ met first, then the Church of the Apostles had their service, and then the Catholics worshipped. It was a tribute to Christians everywhere that Kay and I were made to feel included, and we saw that God's family extends beyond our own denominational lines. People who had been strangers accompanied me for blood draws and grabbed part of my heart.

Kay couldn't understand at first why it was a highlight for me to have my blood drawn at the hospital. I had never before experienced such blatant love, and it came from a deeply spiritual community of older women of color. They treated me (and every other patient) like a precious child. They gave hugs and kisses and prayed with us.

Kay and I received the call that a liver was available on November 1, 2006. When we arrived at the hospital we were initially directed into a waiting room with ten other patients who would also receive an organ from the donor. One person needed a heart, another would get the pancreas, two people needed kidneys, etc. Soon the doctors entered with coolers that bore the gifts of life. Although the donor was never revealed, newspaper accounts told the story of a fireman in Lexington, Kentucky, that had died in the line of duty that day as he led horses out of a burning barn to safety.

The success of the transplant was almost immediate. My memory, which had disappeared into the shroud of "I don't know what I don't know," reappeared as "I know what I don't know." That was scary as well as frustrating, as I relearned reading and math facts and struggled remembering times, places and details of past experiences. These frustrations were more difficult than the physical recovery, as I was convinced that the pain would diminish.

My family's encouragement provided strength when quite frankly, sometimes it seemed like progress was stagnant. We referred to the lung exercises as the Powerball lotto game "Three in a Row."

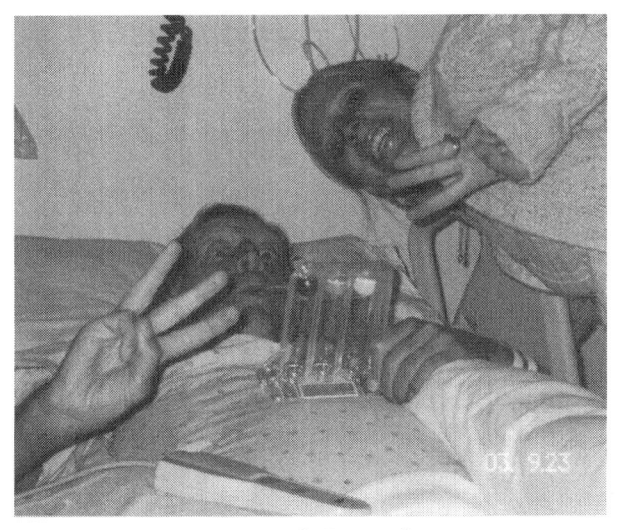

"Three in a Row" with Jaime cheering me on.

Kay and I had a two-bedroom apartment, and the extra room came in handy. We had visitors every week during our six-month stay: family, cousins, friends, coworkers, and even my students and their friends. All who came buoyed our spirits.

What I learned from that convalescence amounted to more than I'd learned in all other adversities. In the past I always thought that I'd been able to persevere because of my passion for life, and that it was up to me to plug through any calamity. This time Kay and I fought the battle together, and we grew because of it. Our dependence upon each other blossomed, and I realized that I desperately needed Kay to get through the rest of my life.

When we returned to Grand Rapids, as part of my recovery, I went to the YMCA for light workouts. Strength returned quickly, and I pushed harder when my surgeons told me to "do what I can." I used the resistance machines and did sit-ups on an incline board. During one such workout in May of 2007, I heard a loud "pop," immediately realizing that I had ripped the incision.

A scan proved the worst, and reconstructive surgery was scheduled for early July, so Kay and I settled in at a nearby hotel in Indianapolis for what we thought would be a quick in-and-out.

My abdominal muscles had been severed to make room for my new liver but these adhesions had ripped, so the muscles had to be painstakingly reattached, layer by layer. Dr. Powellson, the reconstructive surgeon, reported that things looked good but they'd had to "shut me down" for the surgery, and it would take time for my digestive system to function properly. A day passed, and nothing was moving.

Grimly, Dr. Powellson explained that the waste in my body was backing up in my intestines. He said, "We need to get that out." I thought that this would involve something simple, like taking a pill, but he came in with a heavy hose that looked like it had come from a hardware store.

"What's that?" I inquired.

"It's an NG tube," he said. It was to be inserted up my nose, down my throat, and into my stomach so that they could pump the junk out. I panicked. I'd broken my nose a decade ago and never had it repaired, so there was no way that I could allow that hose up my nostril.

Dr. Powellson told Kay to leave the room. As he started to force that monstrous hose up my nose I screamed, "No!" and grabbed his arm to back him off.

Dr.Powellson said, "If that poison doesn't come out, you're going to die, and this is the only way we're going to get it out."

I prayed a quick prayer and let it happen. He had an orderly pin my arms and shoved that hose for all he was worth up my nose, down my throat and fed it into my stomach. I gagged, and projectile vomit went flying. Another orderly cleaned up the mess and before I knew it, a green-black substance started flowing out of the tube into what resembled a huge fishbowl.

This went on for another day, and bowl after bowl was filled. It was agonizing, and for the first time in my life I was ready to quit. At 5:00 a.m. the next morning I prayed, "God, I can't do this any longer. Please take me home."

I thought I was alone, but Kay was in the chair beside me, maintaining her vigil. I heard her voice say, "God, I can't take this any longer either." Both of us were at the end of our ropes.

About thirty minutes later Dr. Powellson appeared and said, "Something woke me up and I felt like I needed to check your progress."

His examination indicated that my fluids had started to move. I wondered if God had let me get to that point of total despair just so I could realize that I could no longer depend on myself. The doctor pulled that hose out of my nose and I could breathe again. He had me get out of bed and start walking and sure enough, the worst had passed.

The kids and my sister Sharon came to visit, and we had our own little 4th of July parade through the hospital. I marched while pushing my fluids stand, and my family walked alongside. We returned home a few days later, and Independence Day had a whole new meaning for us.

About a year after the transplant I had a violent reaction to a new anti-rejection medication. My entire body erupted with hives. Finally Kay took me to the ER at St. Mary's but the staff in Byron Center was not equipped to deal with the severity of the reaction, so we were sent to Indy.

Once admitted, I shared a room with another patient with liver complications. This man, after his first transplant, decided to ignore instructions to abstain from alcohol, and eventually this necessitated another transplant. He again ignored the precautions, and arrived at the hospital fully expecting another transplant. He was dying before my eyes.

As I waited for help my discomfort was so extreme, I wanted to crawl out of my own skin. Then I heard a crystal clear voice say to me, "Be still and know that I am God." Within minutes the doctors entered the room with the news that they knew exactly what had to be done to counteract the reaction.

Continued recovery was a process. Family and friends continued to push me (in a good way), and they encouraged me by providing opportunities in my areas of passion.

30-year award for officiating soccer, MSHAA banquet.

Our friend John Grant had provided invaluable legal advice to Kay over the years. He also pushed me out of feeling sorry for myself by telling me not to be a wimp, and reassured me that I would be fine. I thought he was nuts when he told me I'd ski again.

One day John brought me a picture of a motorcycle with three wheels, knowing that having an additional wheel under my seat would provide more safety and confidence. That made sense, so we had the bike repaired and converted into a trike. Kay and I travelled to Milwaukee, Wisconsin, with our friends, Mart and Mary Hollebeek, to attend the 105th Harley Davison anniversary celebration in August of 2008.

Ironically, my health complications allowed me to connect with my mom like never before. When I was recovering she lived in a care facility because she had Alzheimers. I came to see her not by choice, but out of a sense of duty when my sisters bugged me.

As soon as I'd walk in and say, "Hi, Mom," she'd sometimes become agitated.

She replied the same way each time. "Who are you? Why are you here? Go away. I'm calling the cops."

I'd point to the family picture on the wall. She'd recognize Dad. Then I'd point out Sharon, Donna and me, and she'd say, "I don't have any children. Go away." Then she'd ring for the nurse, and although the nurse knew who I was, she'd say it was best for me to leave.

I'd go home frustrated and tell Kay that it was a waste of my time and that I wasn't going again. I'd return a month or two later and sometimes Mom would say, "Hi, Andy," so I was conflicted.

Kay reminded me about how I got my memory back when I was dealing with encephalopathy. She said, "You had to go back to the events of your past, not the present. It's probably the same with your mom."

The next time, instead of saying, "Hi, Mom," I took "mom" out of the equation and just said, "Hello." She returned my greeting, and I asked her if she'd had a good night.

"Yes, I did. And you?" she answered pleasantly.

I asked if she was married, and she said that she was. I asked where her husband was, and her answer was, "In Germany."

Then it hit me. Of course she doesn't have kids. In her mind, her husband was still serving in World War II.

Sometimes Mom told me things about her childhood that I'd never before heard. She told me she'd gone to school at Grand Rapids Christian High School, and I asked her how she got there, since she lived in the country and there was no bus service. She said she lived with her grandfather who lived across from the school.

I asked if she had a boyfriend. Sometimes the boyfriend was my dad, and she told of when he rode his bike to her farm and asked her father if he could call on her. She stood behind the door and heard my grandpa ask him about his intentions. My father held in his hand a bunch of wildflowers, and Mom even remembered that they were bluebells and daisies. Grandpa allowed them to go for a walk; Mom said that Dad was the most well behaved young man.

There were stories of caroling during the Christmas season. Everyone wanted to be in my dad's group because he could play trumpet, and it was more pleasant to be accompanied rather than sing a capella.

One day I said to her, "Did your husband ever come back from the war?"

"Oh, yes."

When I asked where they lived she promptly replied, "860 10th Street. Our phone number was Glendale 83409."

This was, in fact, the number in Grandma and Grandpa DeVries' house and store where we had lived, the one I called all the time, and the first one I'd memorized.

Mom was "on" that day so I continued. "Did you ever have children?"

She thought and thought and finally said, "We had a son."

Now I was nervous because I didn't know how far to press her. I asked, "When was he born?"

"In the spring of 1947. Spring came early that year. The crocuses were up. We named our boy after my husband: Andrew John DeVries Junior."

I took a huge chance. "That's my name."

Mom looked at me. "I have a son?" She started to cry, and so did I. She said, "My brain is so tired. Will you come back sometime?"

And I remembered when I was going through the recall exercises, working so hard to get my memory back; my brain would hurt, too.

Some days I would visit and it was like a wave had washed over her, and she remembered nothing. It was such a gift that she lived long enough for me to connect with her in this way. This was the first healing.

The second healing occurred when I came the next time and she said, "Hi, Andy." She remembered me. She continued, "Did you ever get married? You didn't marry Valerie, did you? You married that girl from California, Kay. How is that going?"

I said it was great, and that we had three kids.

"I'd love to meet them. You got married in California, didn't you? I remember that wedding."

This seemed like another breakthrough. I asked her how she had traveled, and she said, "We drove."

I asked whom she traveled with. "Dad, Bob and Sharon, and Donna and Al."

My dad had not attended because we had drifted apart, and Bob was in the National Guard, so this was not accurate. My mom, bound and determined to go, had driven out with my sisters and my brother-in-law Al.

I said, "Mom, that's six people. There's no way six people would fit in a car.

"Well, we had the 98 Oldsmobile."

"That's still a lot of people in a car. Where did they sit?"

"Well, Dad drove. I sat next to him, then Sharon."

I said, "Mom, Bob is my size. There's no way he sat in the back."

"You're right. Your dad didn't go. How did you feel about that? I have never been so mad at that man."

She probably had never admitted that to anyone, out of loyalty to him. But her admission vindicated me after years of deep hurt, which allowed me to forgive so much.

The third breakthrough happened on the day that she died in January of 2008. Her respiration was labored and shallow, and she breathed about five times per minute. One of her arms was flopping like limp spaghetti, and I wondered if anything was going on in her brain. I got nose to nose with her, and called out, "Mom!"

Both of her eyes opened wide as saucers and she said, "Hello, son."

I said, "I love you, Mom."

She said, "I love you, Andy." And she died. That was the first time I remembered hearing those words from her.

From this I learned to tell my own kids and my wife often that I love them. I tell the kids who I mentor that I love them. They need to hear it if that is their love language.

Brushes With Death Bring Abundant Life

Four generations: Great Grandma DeVries, Avery Kay and Jaime Ekkens, ADV.

Ties That Bind: Passion, Perseverance and Praise

Philippians 4:13: "I can do all things through Christ who strengthens me."

Past, present and future generations of my family have much more in common than a surname. Reflecting on our life experiences, how we respond, and what we learn and share from these events has affirmed some common characteristics: the ***passion*** that drives us to make a difference, the ***perseverance*** to keep going in the face of adversity, and the desire to give the ***praise*** to God, who has a perfect plan and supplies the necessary strength for us to accomplish all things.

The passions in my own life are the things that I've discovered I'm good at, and they have been shaped by my values and life experiences. It's been important to me to be a good dad and husband; to be a businessman; to further the common good and help others achieve; and to teach, listen, and mentor. When I followed these passions with intensity I made a lot of mistakes, but I kept going because I cared deeply. These things all had to be pursued with perseverance. What motivates me is when someone tells me "no". This fighting spirit has not always served me well, but it has helped me to survive in the darkest valleys. Quitting has not been an option, especially when I have been passionate for a specific cause.

I've had a lot of help. As I look back on my life I realize that, at almost every juncture, God had placed alongside me somebody of influence, someone who made me realize that I could help people and even be instrumental in changing lives. Other people cleared the way for my passions; they gave me hope and sage advice, and when I made mistakes they had the courage to tell me because they cared.

Ken and Jan Bootsma, ADV and Kay.

Whatever strength I have is from God. Every time I had a mountain to climb, the strength and fortitude was not my own. God's providence and grace kept me alive when I did dumb things, and he always put the right person in front of me to keep me from doing things that were absolutely stupid. Faith has been the driving force that has kept me going when I might have otherwise quit, and the responses to God's constant provision are praise and actions.

My first mentor, Bill Carlson.

The person who deserves the most gratitude is my dear wife Kay. In our years together, there were many times that she could have given up on me. I couldn't let that happen. God brought us together, and we could not allow our marriage to fall apart. At one point we asked ourselves what we agreed on. The easy answer was that God had given us three kids whom we loved dearly.

It's no small irony that, after so many years of not getting it right, we recently led a marriage seminar at Hillside Community Church. Our presentation was largely based on the principles that we have discovered in a book called

The Noticer about recognizing and responding to different love languages.

We had waited so long for Jaime, and when she finally arrived we had such big plans for her. She was all we had hoped for, a wonderful child. As an elementary student Jaime missed out on some math fundamentals, and I found her counting on her fingers. Her struggles in math affected other areas. Since Kay and I were teachers we thought we could provide sufficient help, but we accepted help from a tutor, which was money well spent.

Our little girl dug in her heels and decided that she'd be an athlete. Although she was always the smallest girl, there wasn't a sport she didn't play and she gave everything her all. I recently found some pieces from coaches who had written about what an inspiration she'd been to her team. She pushed and pushed.

While I persevered when someone told me "no," Jaime humbly accepted help when she struggled and worked until she beat it. Like her great-Grandma DeVries, if she had fifty cents she quickly turned it into a dollar.

When Jaime turned sixteen and earned her license we bought her a mid-sized Buick that had seen better days. To encourage responsibility Kay and I said that we'd pay for insurance until the kids got a ticket. This worked for a week. On their way to work, Jaime and her friend Denise pulled out of our driveway in Jaime's car. She was distracted and grazed the handlebar of a young boy on a bicycle just a few yards from our house.

He was shaken up and Jaime, distraught, received a ticket. We were sympathetic but rules are rules, and the money she earned from her part time jobs went to pay for insurance. After a few more tickets she couldn't afford to drive.

Jaime was working at Uccello's as a server but needed transportation. I thought a bicycle would work just fine, but Jaime didn't agree and found a way around the rules. She interviewed for and was hired as a nanny for a wonderful family, the Heules, who had five delightful young girls. The bonus was a car and insurance. She became a very careful driver and a wonderful nanny. The relationship with that family remains strong fifteen years later. Jaime learned perseverance her own way.

Jaime married Steve Ekkens in 2002.

I see that same perseverance in the way Jaime works with her children, Avery, Mckenna (Mookie), and Sam. Sam was born with a congenital condition called hypoplastic left heart syndrome (HLHS). When he was born it was discovered that the left side of his heart does not function properly. He has only two chambers in his heart and has undergone countless open heart surgeries, dodging death time after time.

Jaime is a patient and loving mother. She knows that loving her children well is more important than a spotless house. She knows how to make friends and keep friends, cares deeply about those who are in contact with her, and is not afraid to speak her mind with love and conviction.

She still plays soccer and continues to run in 10Ks and 15Ks, even a half-marathon. In May 2013 Kay and I joined the Steve Ekkens family in the Howard Hill Hustle, a 5K benefit for Kalamazoo Christian School. The first three quarters of a mile

Ties That Bind: Passion, Perseverance and Praise

were uphill, and the climb was excruciating. I caught my breath at the summit and finished strong. Although I was only passing senior citizens and young kids at the end, it still felt good when that competitive spirit kicked in.

This was an emotional day because, according to doctors, I would never walk again and my grandson Sam's weak heart would keep him sedentary. Jaime pushed Sam in a stroller and waited for me at the finish line so Sam and I could finish at the same time. As he and I crossed the line together I could not help but think of God's goodness.

Julie was our little girl who cried for her first couple of years. In retrospect, she probably had ear problems and never felt great, but we didn't know that at the time. We learned from her that things don't have to be done right now. Julie would set her own pace, which was not often Kay's or my pace. When she set her mind to something she would get it in gear, and the task would get done and be done well.

As a competitor in swimming Julie did not want to take attention away from the team, and was uncomfortable being identified as someone special. She broke records constantly in practice but did not want to break the school record in a meet because the girl who held it was Lisa Kuiphof, a friend of Jaime's. Once she received permission from Lisa she broke the record time and time again.

I encouraged Julie to pursue a lifesaving certificate so she could find employment as a lifeguard. About the same time, the Sports Xchange began offering swimming lessons and we needed an instructor. I found a great instructor in Kathy Starkweather but she needed help as our enrollment was booming. I suggested that Julie apply. She did, and the two of them hit it off. So many kids signed up to learn swimming from two teachers who really cared that we had to offer extra classes. Julie blossomed before my eyes. I think that may have been what encouraged her to pursue teaching as a calling. She could see the difference she made in people's lives by being patient and caring, two traits that Julie possesses in abundance. Julie is patient in all she does and pursues excellence with a passion.

An example of Julie's quiet perseverance was when she decided to leave home. We came home one day to see a rental truck in the driveway, and Julie announced that since Michigan had no teaching jobs, she was moving to Florida. When it was time to buy her first car she did meticulous research, and carefully drove that Toyota for about ten years.

On the flip side, she could also show incredible spunk when she had all systems go. When we bought Sea-Doos I watched this girl going nuts in the water. It turned out to be our Julie. She has competed in triathlons, combining her swimming prowess with her running.

Julie married Russ Iwema in 2008.

When she and Russ were blessed with their son Jake, he didn't respond as quickly as other babies. Julie did not wring her hands in helplessness, but persevered with him and worked with him, and it paid off. That little boy is so much fun, and what a gift that he was born to such patient parents. In Julie I see love exuding; she is an exceptional teacher and mom.

Drew entered the world running full tilt, and we learned about ADD from him. He kept three balls going at the same time, and they weren't all in the air. We had good counsel from our pediatrician, Dr. Bulten, who helped us understand that not everybody gets the same stations on the radio. A lot of people listen to AM, and they see someone's lips moving to a song but they can't find that song because it's on FM, a totally different band.

Drew was blessed with what Kay and I called his "Drew-ness." We could have tried to force him to fit in a box with everyone else, which would have been a huge mistake. God creates stones and man creates bricks. Bricks are all the same and interchangeable, but stones are not. The beauty of stone rests in what it can do, and because it is so unique. Getting to school on time was a challenge for Drew because of all the other things he had to do. He bought a boat on impulse, and he and his friend Nolan would take it out and fish all day.

He and his friends accept and enjoy the fact that he doesn't dance to the same tunes that others do, and he doesn't see the same type of picture that others do. Drew is special in his willingness to understand that people aren't all the same, and this allows him to pick up perspectives on life that most people miss.

Drew married Evie In'tHout in the winter of 2009. Their son Arie John was born in September, 2012.

Drew sent me an ironic letter recently, saying that much of his confidence comes from the life experiences that we had together. He acknowledged that Kay and I had risked a lot to provide these experiences. Since I had an absent dad, I gave myself life experiences, but it was important that my son have those experiences with me.

Kay and I have tried to be encouraging parents, but we each brought different dynamics into the equation. The kids received words of affirmation, gifts of time, and lots of hugs. As adults they appreciate that when you care for someone, you do things for them.

The book of Proverbs tells us that if we train a child in the way he should go, when he is old he will not depart from it, and we are watching that now. The areas in which we trained our children have also become important to them. They have taught their own children about God, Jesus, and the power of prayer. This is reflected in their choices of schools and churches, and the way they are giving back. The greatest gift is to see a continuum – a common thread – of passion, perseverance and praise in our children.

A Halloween hayride with the grandkids.

Perspective In a Nutshell

"We are all in the same boat, in a stormy sea, and we owe each other a terrible loyalty." — *G.K. Chesterton*

Challenges in life are constant, and each challenge in my life has taught a lesson that I would not have learned otherwise. If this book were further subtitled, the additional word would be "Perspective." I'm thankful that I've been able to gain perspective in the areas of my life that have given me the most joy and have been worth fighting for:

<u>On marriage</u>: Kay and I were so radically different when we married. Even though we were in love, there was an awful lot we did not have in common, and we realized that we had to find ways to work through differences. Kay came from a west coast liberal mentality and I came from a Midwest conservative mentality. I fought with my parents and she didn't. But what makes me proud and content is that we figured it out, and we didn't quit.

A book called <u>The Noticer</u> by Andy Andrews introduced me to the concept of love languages. Simply put, love languages are verbal and non-verbal communications between partners that build a nurturing environment. They include words of affirmation, spending time with a loved one, acts of service, gifts and touch. I learned that I needed to speak Kay's languages of time and acts of service in order to connect with her. Previously I'd thought that everyone spoke the love language of words of affirmation because that's my love language.

Lake Louise, Calgary, 1997.

Our money issues still aren't resolved, but the difference is that now we don't argue. My approach was to earn it first; after you've earned the goal as well as a slush fund, make the purchase. Kay's approach was to buy it now and pay for it later. When she found out I wouldn't buy a car until I could pay cash for it, she was flabbergasted. Although we've both been firm in our stances, we have found that disagreement can be healthy. Put the positives on one side, put the negatives on the other side, and play it out fairly. We've learned to talk through things because we've learned one another's love languages.

One of the benefits of being in a committed, steadfast relationship is that you get to figure things out - together. You go in with your myopic outlook thinking that you must be right, but you find out that the person you love, who has had a totally different upbringing and bank of experiences, is often the one who has the best view of the entire picture.

Perspective in a Nutshell

<u>On parenting</u>: My theory is that our lives can be divided into four distinct stages. We enter the world into the stage of captivity. This is by no means a pejorative term; the parents' important job is to teach values and morals to children at this stage. When a child in captivity makes an age-appropriate decision, parents need to cut some slack and give the child a bit more rope. When the child makes an age-inappropriate decision the parent must pull in the reins, tighten the rope, and lessen the area of responsibility because the child has demonstrated that it has not been earned.

As a child grows and becomes accomplished in learning the parents' values and morals, more independence is gained until parents decide that it's proper to cut the child loose. During this stage of independence the young adult searches for the mate who is a good match and has similar values.

The new couple chooses and assumes the best characteristics of each side, and together they become interdependent. They grow together, choose wisely, and make good decisions based on what they have picked up from their partner. This continues until they have a child of their own.

Now the new parents begin their role as captors. It is their turn to teach and train values and morals, and at the appropriate time the child is released to independence.

In the fourth stage, the legacy stage, parents of independent children reflect on what has been learned and taught. They attempt to live the rest of their lives helping their independent children, not as teachers but as supporters. They listen and watch and offer occasional suggestions about grandchildren and life situations, but they keep learning, and they pray that what they've learned, those common threads from past generations, can be passed on so that their story won't be lost.

<u>On being a grandparent</u>: When I held our babies, as well as experiencing indescribable joy, I felt an overwhelming responsibility because of the realization that we had about eighteen years to get it right. We intensely experienced every one of our children's highs and lows along the way.

My grandkids are not my children; I have learned that I can't force my way or will on them. I also cut them more slack than I did my own kids. Once they have made a choice I need to support them and give affirmation when needed.

The responsibility of raising my grandkids belongs to my children. If they have questions about parenting they can ask, but I need to stay out of the way. We share the grandparent role with other couples, so we need to be equitable. We're all doing the best we can to ensure that these kids go into the world well adjusted, and that someone will always have their back.

Perspective in a Nutshell

Anna Maria Island, Spring Break, 2011.

    Avery has a huge heart; it's important to her that others are taken care of. We never know what Mookie is thinking; she's more deliberate and methodical. Sam is a fighter. We thought he was lost so many times, but time and time again he shows passion and perseverance.

    Jake watches and watches, and when we see his smile it makes everything worthwhile. Arie has also been a fighter through his surgeries. We look forward to seeing the individual personalities of each grandchild develop as they grow.

    I want all of my grandkids to know that they have unlimited potential. God has a plan for them and will give them the necessary strength to carry out that plan. As long as Kay and I are alive we will support them in that quest for unlimited potential and do everything we can to make certain that the education they receive, the experiences they have, and the friends they make help them reach their goals.

July, 2013.

The only thing left on my bucket list is to live long enough to see my grandkids graduate, marry, and have kids of their own.

<u>On teaching</u>: When it comes to sources of inspiration, many people can point to stories from books and movies, or to music or art. But I gained inspiration from the underdog. It's been powerful, time and time again, to find someone who didn't have a chance and to help them find a way to become successful. More than anything else I think of how the underdog has motivated me to provide opportunities for others.

I learned early and was reminded often that if a child could not learn, it was because I wasn't teaching in a language that they understood. As a teacher I became the student, and I think that all good teachers have a responsibility to teach in a way that students can learn. I encountered too many teachers who became frustrated with students, who said kids were not trying hard enough, or that they were lazy. Teachers need to be willing to break out of the box.

Some people can learn from observing others' mistakes, but

unfortunately, firsthand experience has always been my most effective teacher. Because I didn't have a strong relationship with my own father, I found my own way, and in the process I probably made every mistake possible. In most cases once was enough to prevent repetition. It is my hope that I can prevent others from making the same missteps.

My sisters, cousins and I set up a scholarship at Calvin College in the names of our parents to provide an education for kids whose parents did not have an opportunity to attend college. One of the requirements is that the student be willing to be mentored. Through this, I've learned that lots of kids have a tremendous need for stability, love, and a relationship of trust.

On decision-making: In my childhood, decisions were made based on fear of being spanked. When it came to asking for advice, I learned that kids my age would make the same foolish decisions, so I was always seeking an older, wiser mentor.

When making decisions it's important to reflect on past situations to gain a big picture perspective. If experience and common sense are lacking, I go to someone who has more.

Go to the experts, depending on the area in which advice is needed. When it comes to money decisions, I find someone successful. When there is a nurturing decision I go to Kay because she has an amazing capability of depth in relationships. She sees things differently, and that's exactly why I go to her.

When decisions may have a permanent effect on me and those I love, I go to God in prayer. He gives advice through his Word and through experiences.

In my work with Calvin students and whenever someone asks for help with a decision, I have found a consistent model to be effective.

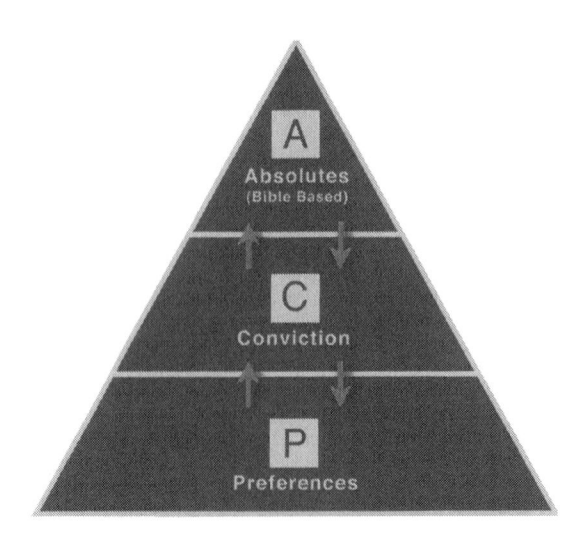

```
        A
    Absolutes
   (Bible Based)

        C
    Conviction

        P
    Preferences
```

The "A" stands for absolutes, or biblical truths that can't be argued. The "C" stands for convictions, which emanate from absolutes. We make many decisions based on conviction because of the absolutes that we picked up as children when we were taught values and morals. The "P" stands for preferences that we invoke when we have to make a decision about something that may affect us either in the long or short term.

For example, if a young man is wrestling with smoking pot, his preference is to continue to bow to peer pressure. At the same time he is feeling convictions, which stem from his parents' pressure for him to stop. The biblical component, or the absolute, is that we are called to view our bodies as temples of the Holy Spirit.

Turning back down to the conviction component, if God has given him this body, then what the young man does with it should be pleasing to his creator. If he smokes weed is he building his body or tearing it down? That becomes the conviction. Preferences are now easier to carry out because they are in line with values and morals that have been taught since childhood.

Perspective in a Nutshell

<u>*On living life to the fullest*</u>: Kay challenged me about six months ago by suggesting that I was "living to die rather than living to live." We were talking about moving to a place with more sun exposure, as our condo has a northern exposure and not a single window that lets in sunlight. This can be a bit depressing if sunlight is important in your life. My response was, "Turn some lights on." Of course this didn't sit well with Kay.

I pondered her remark and came across an account of the life cycle of the eagle. Eagles have a life expectancy of forty years, and at the end of this span their talons harden and their beaks hook, preventing them from eating and preening their feathers, and soon they can no longer fly. However, if they bang their beaks against a rock to break off the hook, their life cycle can be extended for thirty years.

I had become comfortable with life and was going through the motions. Kay was right. The guy she married didn't live like that; he lived for challenges. It hit me pretty hard. I decided then and there that I was not going to sit around waiting to die, but was going to rejuvenate, like the eagle.

I sent the eagle story to Kay and our children and vowed to get the spring back in my step. We are now planning to move to a home with a southern exposure overlooking the golf course. Even though the move is across the street, new energy is flowing and the eagle will fly again.

In addition to making the decision to move, I began working out at the YMCA with the idea of trying to learn how to run. It's not pretty, but I have rehabbed enough to be able to move a bit faster than walking. I was able to officiate three high school soccer games in the spring of 2013. I didn't tell the athletic directors, the coaches or the other officials that I couldn't run and let them think that I was just old and slow. The games went very well, and years of experience came back quickly to allow me to work effectively.

On shifting values: Life experiences, especially in the past two decades, have influenced my values. What I treasure most now is relationships and experiences. Things are not important to me anymore, which is a radical shift from my younger self. I wanted good skis, good golf clubs, good clothes, a nice house and powerful cars. Now a car is a way to get somewhere. Any club can hit a ball. But it is who I visit with the car and who I play golf with that's important.

Chuck Stoddard, Dr. Tom Duthler, Henry Bouma, ADV.

ADV and Ed Huizinga, Merion Golf Course, PA, 2005.

Perspective in a Nutshell

I've had the good fortune to play on two dozen of the top 100 ranked golf courses in the world with wonderful friends who share my love of the game. As well as international courses we've played on Pinehurst #2 in North Carolina; Winged Foot in New York; Oakmont in Pennsylvania; Crystal Downs and Oakland Hills in Michigan; Muirfield Village and Inverness in Ohio; Spyglass Hill in California, and Black Diamond in Florida.

Relationships are at a premium and can't be bought. Life is about being the best we can be as we follow God's plan and prepare ourselves for a better place. This would be impossible if we did not develop relationships and learn from and help others as they walk the same road.

If there's a grudge hanging out there, it's impossible to build that relationship. After all these years I think I've learned to apologize quickly. I also try to forgive and forget quickly.

I have, since my accident, learned what a thankful heart is all about. Kay and I reflected about the people who have been instrumental in our lives, and I was motivated to go back and thank them all: professors at Calvin, friends, even competitors.

If there's one person who didn't receive adequate thanks, it was my Grandma DeVries. When I was breaking away from my parents and trying to become independent I also started to pull away from Grandma. When she was in the rest home lying in bed, I didn't visit her enough. I've learned that when kids are not loved properly in childhood, they have a rough road ahead of them, and my grandma provided that security for me. I look forward to meeting her in heaven and saying, "Thanks, Grandma."

Prior to the accident there were many occasions in which I laughed so hard I couldn't breathe. Now I smile more. Having the accident has mellowed me and taken the edge off the extremes.

If you've been a social drinker and you stop drinking, you see things through a different prism. When my liver condition was diagnosed, I realized that any alcohol consumption would be a nail in my coffin. I experienced a big change in the dynamics at social gatherings. In the parties I've been to in the last decade I've watched what happens. The guys congregate and talk about something that ties them: activities such as sports or politics, or things related to nature. Rarely will a female join the discussion. Women's topics revolve around nurture. They typically discuss family and relationships.

These days I feel more comfortable with the women. Since my brushes with death I am more at ease with their social language. It's changed how my antenna focuses and it took all that time lying on my back without much hope to figure it out. Although I still enjoy sports, I now look for the backstories. The athlete is fascinating, but I want to know what the wife of the warrior is thinking and how it all weaves together.

Being involved with the ROMEOs (Really Old Men Eating Out) has provided both learning opportunities and a way to get to know other men of completely different backgrounds. This group was formed two decades ago by local professionals looking for an excuse to discuss items of importance where they would be unencumbered by time or personal constraints.

Other group members include a Mormon bishop, a Jewish rabbi, a CPA, a ping pong Olympian, a factory owner, a judge, a hospital administrator, and a lawyer. The rules are simple. There are enough men to have a great debate each month. One person picks the restaurant and a discussion topic. We've debated everything from people of influence to our bucket lists. We talk about how we want to be remembered and events that changed the world. All opinions are challenged, so we need to come prepared. Notes are taken and produced for the next meeting.

This group has moved me out of my comfort zone, and I have to read and research before I attend the meetings. Once in a while we include our spouses - this is always fascinating because we really don't know each other outside of this setting, so hearing our wives' perspectives is illuminating.

My cousins and I have been involved in an investment group since 1990. To honor Grandpa Rodenhouse we named the group AGN after the scripture ("A good name is rather to be chosen than riches...") that was above the doorframe of his business. We donate the earnings to a family member in need or in memory of a relative who passes on. Since my cousins are pilots we try to fly somewhere together and have flown a number of times to the Experimental Aircraft Association (EAA) in Oshkosh, Wisconsin, for the annual fly-in where we see hundreds of planes.

The AGN Investment Group, Oshkosh, Wisconsin, 1998.

On some trips to Oshkosh we rough it by sleeping under the wings in sleeping bags. In one especially memorable year, three of us rode our motorcycles to the fly-in and met other cousins who had flown in.

<u>On my own parents</u>: I can only share stories about my parents' families because of a relatively new sense of perspective.

I regret that I didn't have a relationship with my dad. I wish I knew who his friends were and what made him tick; what made him successful and happy; what frustrated him.

A couple months ago an older gentleman approached me and asked, "You're Andy DeVries, aren't you?"

This man and my father had served as church elders many years ago. I asked him to tell me what my father was like, and he said that my dad was one of the finest men with whom he had worked. Hearing this was an unexpected gift. Since my father and I had a contentious relationship, it is important for me to realize that he made many positive contributions. As the son of immigrants, my father did not get to choose his circumstances. He doggedly served his family and his country. I think that so much was expected of him at an early age, and because he delivered so well he expected the same of me. Besides a strong work ethic, I also learned fiscal responsibility from him, and how to be generous with my time. I can't wait to meet my dad in heaven.

Although my mom did not express her love in words, she was telling me all along that she loved me, but not in a language that I understood. My mom's love language was actions and deeds. As soon as I shed my dirty clothes she washed them in her washtub with the rippled washboard. Then she painstakingly hung the clothes on the line outside, and when they were dry she

Perspective in a Nutshell

ironed them. She even ironed my underwear. I didn't care if my things were ironed; sometimes I would intentionally wrinkle things and she would cry.

The Rodenhouse family: Bob and Connie, Mom, Ken, Al and Eleanor, ADV.

Mom needed to be loved through actions and deeds, but regrettably, my father and I were not familiar with that language. On Easter Sunday all the moms wore corsages to church that had been lovingly presented by their families. My mom sported a corsage just like the rest of the ladies, but the difference was that she bought her own. She also purchased her own card. The few times I cut forsythias or lilacs for her from the bushes in the yard, she was overwhelmed with joy.

My independence was due in part to my mother's willingness to let me go. She cried so hard when I hitchhiked to Florida, and revealed later to me that she thought she'd never see me again, but she did not stand in the way. As I found out in the last years of her life, she may not have always agreed with my dad, but she was loyal and steadfast.

I am convinced that my ancestors' positive qualities were common threads that have also been woven into the tapestry of my sisters' lives.

The 1936 Rodenhouse truck. Sharon, Kay and ADV, 2013.

Unlike me, Sharon had a great relationship with our father. She could make a dollar go further than anyone I knew and was never afraid to be an individual. Sharon has been a dedicated teacher for over forty years. She started at West Side Christian, and our teams would compete against one another when I was at Jenison Christian. She then continued at Creston Christian and now teaches at Rockford Christian.

A walk in Sharon's back yard is proof of her love for nature and the environment, and she transmits that to her students by getting them involved at Blandford Nature Center and Calvin's Ecosystem Preserve. She is an exceptional mom.

Donna married Al Hoeksema, one of the first to graduate with a Bible degree from Calvin College. For a while they were missionaries in the Yucatan. Al died young of a brain tumor, leaving Donna with four young children. A true fighter, she worked out a deal with the school to work as Administrative Secretary for the Superintendent in exchange for Christian education for her children. She came back strong, eventually marrying a fine man named Curt Vellenga.

Maybe Donna's hardships encouraged her to become a champion for

Perspective in a Nutshell

the underdog. She ran homes for unwed mothers in Bradenton, Florida, for fifteen years. It started when one woman took in an unmarried pregnant girl and Donna got involved. Eventually three homes were dedicated to caring for these unwed mothers. Along with helping them become effective mothers, the staff helped them earn their GEDs and develop work habits.

On how we impact others: A book titled Making Hope Happen was sent to me in March 2013 by the author, Shane Lopez. I was surprised to see that part of my life story had been featured in the book. Lopez references others as well and writes about what the stories have in common:

"I consider these people to be charter members of the tribe of Super-Empowered, Hopeful Individuals, or SEHIs - people who believe the future will be better than the present - for everyone - and that they can make it happen. They believe that changing the world is a realistic goal despite every obstacle imaginable. They spread hope every day.

Most of us are like Andy. If we have a vision and plan for the future, we can't help but be pulled forward by life, even when our present betrays us. We start to create a narrative about a future self that competes with the old stories about ourselves. As we fill in more details and take small steps in our future direction, our energy is freed up. When we're excited about "what's next," we invest more in our daily life, and we can see beyond current challenges."

An interesting takeaway from Lopez' book has been the concept of "futurecasting," which entails imagining a future goal and understanding the steps that are required to achieve it. Often it takes other people in your life to

205

push you into seeing things clearly.

Since I did not grow up hearing words of love, it was tough for me to vocalize my feelings. Blake Forslund was the first man to whom I said, "I love you," and I felt way out of my comfort zone. I never cried so hard as I did when my dear friend died in 2012.

Blake's widow Joan recently sent me a letter, and her beautiful words caught me off guard. She thanked me for being a special spiritual friend to Blake and said that he and I had mentored one another. I had always thought that I was on the receiving end, and it was humbling to hear that our relationship had been reciprocal.

Just as we cannot accurately predict how another person can influence us, we are also often unaware of how we impact others; but that's one reason to make the most of every situation.

Refusing to lose and knowing that God has a plan have kept me going forward. It's like climbing a steep dune. If you're determined, you can get to the top. If you quit you'll never get anywhere. It may be two steps forward and one step back, it may be a lateral move, but determination brings steady progress. Although God has a plan, it's up to us to make choices regarding how to carry it out. God gives us free will, and every time we make a bad choice or a mistake there's room to learn.

When attempting to look forward in the midst of a hardship, it's difficult to see how some situations can ever bring goodness, but getting through the trauma brings wisdom and understanding. After you've made it to the other side you can look back and say, "Aha, that's why it happened."

Having been able to live a rich, full life, I can say that God's plan is now so clear; I know that I'm part of the plan, and it's a bigger plan than I could've imagined. When I envision how common threads of generations have been interwoven, I fully believe that there's a God who cares and loves and is worthy of abundant praise.

Bibliography

1. *Holland America Line: A History of Distinction, Innovation and Growth.* **www.maritimeexecutive.com.**

2. *Battle of the Bulge.* **www.history.com.**

3. *Crossing the Rhine February – April 1945.* **www.worldwar2database.com.**

4. *American Experience: Victory in the Pacific.* **www.pbs.com.**

5. Greenberg, Milton. The G.I. Bill of Rights- U.S. Department of State. *Historians in America.*

6. *The History of Baseball in Grand Rapids.* **www.milb.com.**

7. *Sputnik: The Fiftieth Anniversary.* **www.history.nasa.com.**

8. *Mining Anthracite.* **www.explorepahistory.com.**

9. *Apollo 11: First Man on the Moon.* **www.space.com.**

10. *A Brief History of the Links.* **www.oldcourse-experience.com.**

11. *A Foundation Built on a Parent's Perspective.* **www.nha.com.**

History of Dutch Surnames

Holland had, since 1806, been under the rule of Napoleon Bonaparte's brother, King Louis (Lodewijk) Bonaparte. Unhappy with his brother's permissive rule of Holland and his lack of enforcement of the ban on trade and shipping between Holland and Great Britain, Napoleon abolished the Kingdom of Holland in 1810, annexed it and placed it under French rule.

While Napoleon plundered Holland and eventually left it in economic shambles, he and his brother instituted civil reforms, codes and laws that would form the basis for much of the Netherlands' future civil law. Louis established a monetary system using the Guilder. On August 18, 1811, Napoleon decreed the mandatory registration of births, deaths and marriages, and compulsory military service. According to the decree, in part:

Those of our subjects of the Departments of the former Holland... who until now have not had fixed surnames and given names, must adopt them during the year, and declare them before the officers of the civil registry... where they reside...Those having known surnames... will be excepted.

According to historians, at the beginning of the 19th century most Dutch inhabitants already had a family name although they were not legally required. The Dutch traditionally used a "patronymic" system in which the father's first name became the first son's last name. Gradually in the 1600s, people began to turn the patronymic name into modern last names: Jan Hendricksen (Jan the son of Hendrick) gave his son the surname Hendricksen instead of Jansen. A suffix was often added to indicate 'son of' or 'daughter of.' For example, Jan, son of Hendrick would be written Jan Hendricks, Jan Hendrickse or Jan Hendricksen." There was a similar system for women's names.

Thousands of Dutch people had no "proper" family names. As a result of the establishment of mandatory and official registration of births, marriages and deaths and for purposes of the census, the Dutch who did not have "fixed surnames and given names" were required to adopt a permanent family name. Some surnames refer to qualities of people, like De Jong (the younger) but also De Groot (the big) or Dik (fat). There are many geographic related names like De Vries (from Friesland) and Van den Berg (from the mountains), even though there are no mountains at all in Holland. A third group is formed by the occupations: Bakker (baker), Visser (fisher) and DeBoer (farmer).

Many patronymics did become permanent family names—such as today's very common Peters, Jansen, Willems, etc. Consistent with the Dutch independent mind, pragmatism, stubbornness, and sense of humor, thousands of Dutch did not take Napoleon seriously. Perhaps they even wanted to mock Napoleon and his system. Additionally, they looked at this "name system" as a temporary law that would be repealed once Napoleon left Holland.

So, they deliberately adopted and registered family names that are funny, ridiculous, confusing, and sometimes even lewd—many at the expense of Napoleon and the French occupiers. Examples include Spring in 't Veld (jump in the Field), Uiekruier (onion-crier), Naaktgeboren (born naked), Poepjes (little sh*t), Schooier (tramp), Piest ([he] urinates), and Rotmensen (rotten people). Also, De Keizer (the emperor) was chosen by some to mock Napoleon himself.

- The Moderate Voice

Man keeps promise after physician's assistant inspired him to walk again.

GRAND RAPIDS — Following his doctors' protocol, Andy DeVries took a black Sharpie and drew a line across his left thigh. Then, he signed and dated it. And said goodbye to it. He had been injured in a motorcycle accident, so seriously that, on that September day in 2002, his family was called together to bid him farewell — wife Kay and their three children included, Jaime, Julie and Drew. In the week after the crash, Andy somehow dodged death. But he was facing life without a leg.

And just when he couldn't feel any worse, in walked a smiling face asking "Andy, what kind of golf ball do you play?" It was his physician's assistant, Sarah Scholl, and DeVries remembers thinking, "That had to have been the dumbest question you've ever heard."

Still, he answered it, telling Scholl, "I like to play a Titleist Pro V1 when I can find one," given that it's a relatively expensive ball.

When he awoke the next day in his bed at Spectrum Health Butterworth Hospital, there in the midst of a room full of flowers was a 12-pack of yellow V1s. And in that moment, Andy DeVries realized that Sarah Scholl hadn't merely brought him golf balls. She had ushered in hope.

If this story sounds familiar, you heard DeVries relate it to you in person sometime in the past seven years, or you heard it Friday morning on National Public Radio.Andy DeVries thought his love of playing golf would come to an end after nearly losing a leg due to a motorcycle accident several years ago. As part of its ongoing project entitled "StoryCorps," which so far has chronicled the sagas of about 50,000 Americans, NPR broadcast Andy DeVries' tale Friday. At the urging of a friend, DeVries spent about 40 minutes taping with NPR staff parked in an Airstream outside the Grand Rapids Public Museum.

The bus has been recording stories here since Sept. 24, and ends its stay in Grand Rapids this afternoon.

DeVries works in development for Calvin College, though I knew him long before he secured that job, when we played on the same recreational soccer team more than 20 years ago.

I'd lost touch with him but had always known him as an active guy who, among other things, played volleyball with as much zeal as nearly any collegiate athlete. I also wrote a column some years back in which his son Drew figured positively and prominently.

As it turns out, surgeons discovered enough blood flowing to DeVries' toes that they decided not to amputate his leg back in 2002. That I knew. But the lessons imparted by his physician's assistant were something I was unaware of until NPR broadcast his story. We spoke Friday morning just after the segment aired, and I asked Andy, who is now 62, to fill me in. He explained that he developed a close relationship with Scholl while he recovered at Spectrum. In fact, when he was transported from there to another facility for rehabilitation, Scholl wrested Andy's wheelchair from a colleague so she could pilot him to the waiting ambulance.

But, before parting, she asked him to do her a favor. Her father had died before she had the opportunity to get married — and would Andy walk her down the aisle? He reminded her that she didn't even have a boyfriend, something he learned during their conversations.

"Someday I will," she told him.

Then, they parted, with Andy considering that, in her special and subtle way, Sarah had once again injected hope into his life. That he would walk again. For himself and for others. She showed him that he might golf again. And, now, she was adding another layer of sunshine.

'What I learned ... is to give hope.'

Her role in his life so affected him, that Andy has worked since then in conjunction with local doctors and others in an effort to sensitize them to what med schools might not cover.

"You're taught how to slice and dice and take out the bad and make way for the good, but what I learned from Sarah is to give hope," Andy said.

Last spring — nearly seven years after first meeting her — Andy received an e-mail from Sarah, 39, who makes her home in West Linn, Ore., about 20 miles south of Portland. She wrote that she was engaged to Dan Silvernail, 42, and were to be married on June 20. Would he come? She graduated in 1987 from West Ottawa High School and lost her father the year before. Her mother, Joan Scholl, along with many relatives, still lives in the GR area. Sarah now works at Oregon Health & Science University, primarily with cardiac patients "who are at their sickest and in their most desperate hour."

Her philosophy of delivering medical care? "I always try to think 'How would I want my family to be treated?'"

Andy had alerted her earlier to the fact that their story would air on Friday, and she logged onto NPR Thursday evening to read his story online. When she heard Andy's voice delivering the tale before dawn Friday while on her way to work, "I was really overwhelmed," and brought to tears.

Her reaction to the story? "I've now realized that little things — like golf balls — can have a big impact on people."

Sarah met Andy at the airport, and she was sobbing as he strolled up to hug her. It was the first time she had ever seen him walk.

- *The Grand Rapids Press*, October 17, 2009.

ADV golfing with the ball that had been Sarah's gift.

ALUMS SUPPORT 'AVERAGE JOE'

The first year that the Average Joe Scholarship was awarded at Calvin, there were only four applicants. Turns out average Joes don't look for scholarships because they don't think there's anything available for them.

And that's the intent, according to Joe Westra '06, who established the scholarship to recognize ordinary students. "I thought there were plenty of scholarships for people who get really good grades or who are good at music or something else; I wanted to reward somebody who hasn't done anything exceptional but still works really hard."

The Average Joe Scholarship requires a GPA of less than 3.2 (it does require a minimum of 2.7). Other criteria include being a business major, highly motivated and entrepreneurial.

"It's nice to be able to reward a hard-working student with a scholarship, who normally wouldn't qualify for one based on their academic record," said Lynne Heerema, assistant director of financial aid. "This scholarship makes that possible."

And many students fit the criteria. "There are tons of people out there who didn't get straight As that end up in really successful careers," said Westra, who is a regional sales manager for Systems Components in Denver, Colo.

In fact, two of them—Drew DeVries '06 and Chris Hofstra '06— are good friends of Westra's and have joined him in supporting this scholarship.

"Joe and I share a lot of similarities in personality and approach to life," DeVries said. *"When I heard about this scholarship I was on board because Calvin College is a cool place, and I love what I got out of it. I think this fits the profile of what I think a successful student can be; I resonated with the whole style of it. It's for somebody who is academically good enough."*

DeVries, who recently sold his first business and is working on a second business venture, admits he would have fit the criteria for this scholarship. "I got Bs and Cs, which wasn't good enough to be recognized for anything," he said. "But a GPA is not always a direct measure of someone's intelligence; it can be measured in so many different ways."

"My long-term hope," said Westra, *"is that this scholarship provides other people with something to think about and consider in terms of how they might be able to support Calvin and contribute to the hard work of students in some way they can relate to."*

-- Calvin College <u>Spark</u>, Summer 2012

Made in the USA
Lexington, KY
28 June 2014